Cambridge El

CW00566996

Elements in Public and Nonprofit Administration
edited by
Andrew Whitford
University of Georgia
Robert Christensen
Brigham Young University

PUBLIC ADMINISTRATION AND DEMOCRACY

The Complementarity Principle

Anthony M. Bertelli
Pennsylvania State University and Institut Barcelona d'Estudis Internacionals

Lindsey J. Schwartz
Denison University

Shaftesbury Road, Cambridge CB2 8EA, United Kingdom

One Liberty Plaza, 20th Floor, New York, NY 10006, USA

477 Williamstown Road, Port Melbourne, VIC 3207, Australia

314–321, 3rd Floor, Plot 3, Splendor Forum, Jasola District Centre,
New Delhi – 110025, India

103 Penang Road, #05–06/07, Visioncrest Commercial, Singapore 238467

Cambridge University Press is part of Cambridge University Press & Assessment,
a department of the University of Cambridge.

We share the University's mission to contribute to society through the pursuit of
education, learning and research at the highest international levels of excellence.

www.cambridge.org
Information on this title: www.cambridge.org/9781009217606

DOI: 10.1017/9781009217613

First published 2022

A catalogue record for this publication is available from the British Library.

ISBN 978-1-009-21760-6 Paperback
ISSN 2515-4303 (online)
ISSN 2515-429X (print)

Cambridge University Press & Assessment has no responsibility for the persistence
or accuracy of URLs for external or third-party internet websites referred to in this
publication and does not guarantee that any content on such websites is, or will
remain, accurate or appropriate.

Public Administration and Democracy

The Complementarity Principle

Elements in Public and Nonprofit Administration

DOI: 10.1017/9781009217613
First published online: December 2022

Anthony M. Bertelli
Pennsylvania State University and Institut Barcelona d'Estudis Internacionals

Lindsey J. Schwartz
Denison University

Author for correspondence: Anthony M. Bertelli, bertelli@psu.edu

Abstract: This Element argues for a complementarity principle – governance values should complement political values – as a guide for designing the structures and procedures of public administration. It argues that the value-congruity inherent in the complementarity principle is indispensable to administrative responsibility. It identifies several core democratic values and critically assesses systems of collaborative governance, representative bureaucracy, and participatory policymaking in light of those values. It shows that the complementarity principle, applied to these different designs, facilitates administrative responsibility by making the structures themselves more consistent with democratic principles without compromising their aims. This Element is also available as Open Access on Cambridge Core.

Keywords: public administration, democratic theory, political philosophy, social equity, collaborative and participatory governance

ISBNs: 9781009217606 (PB), 9781009217613 (OC)
ISSNs: 2515-4303 (online), 2515-429X (print)

Contents

1 Introduction

After less than three years of service on the Civil Aeronautics Board (CAB), Louis Hector was fed up. In his resignation letter dated September 10, 1959, he did not tell President Eisenhower that he and his colleagues could not do the job of regulating civil aviation that the CAB was meant to do. Instead, he argued that his agency, an independent commission, "is not competent" to do that job (Hector 1960, 931).[1] The CAB was, in his view, "a creature imprisoned by its own structure and procedures. It is unable to form clear policy. It is unable to make sound and comprehensive plans. It is unable to administer its affairs with vigor and dispatch" (931). Worse still, Hector argued that "[t]he policies and plans of the CAB are not coordinated with those of other agencies of our government; they are not responsive to the general policies of the President" (931). Regulatory policymaking untethered from representatives of the people is not done to implement the laws, and with them the goals established by representatives in legislation. It is, he contended, an undemocratic amalgam of judicial, legislative, and executive authority. In closing, Hector recommended that the CAB, which would operate for another twenty-six years, be disbanded, and its three authorities be given to three separate agencies.

The matter of Hector's claim was that the CAB – by virtue of its structure, not the people who serve on it – cannot create a national transportation policy on behalf of the public. What policies it did advance got shaped and reshaped into a collective incoherence by the appeals of stakeholders to a board possessed of sharply divided interests (Hector 1960, 933–937). And when adjudicating claims about routes by air carriers, for instance, the commission, wrote Hector to the President, was "long on judicial form and short on judicial substance" (931). Hector thought that the CAB was not designed for "efficient" policymaking, but we think that his concerns could have been stated even more strongly: The CAB was not suited for the particular representative democracy in the United States. The commission's decision-making independence attenuates the accountability of elected representatives. Adversarial procedures regarding route claims limit pluralism. Democratic values that are fundamental to the American political system were recast inside the structure of the commission.

---

[1] In an article in the *Yale Law Journal*, which began with his letter to the President, Hector (1960, 932) elaborated his reasoning in support of this thesis: "The most important responsibility of an economic regulatory agency such as the CAB is the formulation of broad plans and general policies to ensure that the regulated segment of the economy operates for the public benefit as defined by Congress. This is more important than the decision of specific litigated cases. Planning and policymaking, however, when entrusted to an independent commission, are often accomplished with appalling inefficiency."

Public administration shapes representative government. If the actions that public administrators take to advance public policies that political representatives have decided to pursue through legislation and the structure of the organizations that carry it out can, indeed, impact the values of a representative democracy, it is prudent to consider how it ought to do so. At issue are the democratic values embedded in representative government, those embedded in the structures of public administration, and how these sets of values correspond to one another.

In *Democracy Administered*, Bertelli (2021) advances the normative principle that a good governance structure – that is, an administrative arrangement of rules and procedures, such as a bureaucratic or quasi-governmental organization – is one that facilitates responsible administrative action. He contends that responsible policy work is that done to complement, rather than contradict, the values of a representative democracy. Thus, when a system of government, such as that in the United Kingdom, places a high premium on accountability, the design of governance structures should also privilege that value. Working within those structures, public administrators have an obligation to reinforce the democratic values of the system they serve as long as they do not act beyond their authority. In this way, public administration can "administer democracy." While it sets out this argument, that book does not explicitly argue in support of its indispensability. The purpose of this essay is to supply that argument and, in so doing, to bring alternative claims about "democratic" public administration into discourse with it.

Theorizing a "complementarity principle" – public administration should reinforce the democratic values of that system of representative government it serves (Bertelli 2021, 197) – is crucially important for several reasons. First, existing claims that public administration should "represent" the interests of citizen-clients rest on extra-democratic considerations. Social equity is such a consideration. We remove from this concept some ambiguity about what scholars and practitioners intend, revealing a democratic value that we call fidelitous representation. Second, because representation legitimates the modern state (Bertelli 2021, 178); the question of who is represented within the public administration becomes a crucial matter. With our argument that the represented interests should be those of the whole demos, we challenge various practical claims that would bring the public back into the administrative process on grounds of representation to highlight what can be done to maintain democracy. Third, theorizing value-congruity leads to definitions of democracy and democratic responsibility that can help to guide scholars and practitioners as they advocate strategies for and perform the work of the modern state. Our project is constructive, but that means we must be critical of literatures that propose ways to resolve persistent social ills. To be sure, our critique is focused on their claims to preserving or enhancing democracy, not on the socially valuable intent of the practices they advocate. Adhering to the complementarity principle provides strategies that contributors to these literatures can employ in order avoid shortcutting democratic values in material and impactful ways.

In this essay, we motivate the claim that those who are tasked with designing governance structures ought to adhere to the complementarity principle in their design choices. We first present an argument that value-congruity – the congruence of democratic values in a system of government and its public administration – is indispensable to good governance, which can be understood as conducting public administration in a way that is responsible to citizens. We then articulate and defend a substantive conception of responsible policy work, and we show that failing to expressly aim for value-congruity in institutional design often results in bad – that is, irresponsibly administered – governance. In the process, we unearth a taxonomy of democratic values and use these to articulate a working definition of democracy. We conclude by reiterating the details of the complementarity principle and explain how it serves its purpose.

A note on our presentation style is warranted. Our argument is presented and defended in a "philosophical" style that may seem overly abstract or otherwise foreign to some students of public administration. Yet we proceed in this way to avoid falling prey to what we identify as a common problem of inductive reasoning. Commissioner Hector did this in his resignation letter by claiming that because no independent commission in 1959 can make "clear policy," independent commissions should not be charged with making policy. We aim to argue that the complementarity principle is a general one, useful for designing governance structures in any system of government. We cannot do that by relying on what we now know, for instance, about the world's representative democracies. We will indeed critique some of the leading claims about democratic public administration for employing inductive normative reasoning.

To make our presentation more accessible, we use a fictional dialogue between President Eisenhower and Louis Hector to illustrate important features of our argument. Our style, then, is meant to bring the rigor of a philosophical argument to readers in the public administration community in a way that allows them effectively to use and to critique the complementarity principle. We are frustrated with the disconnection between contemporary political philosophy and normative work within the scholarly field of public administration (see, e.g., Zacka 2022). We hope that our argument will generate a robust discussion among scholars of public administration and policy on the merits of complementarity in the design of governance structures and in the conduct of public administration. We hope that political philosophers will engage it also, moving toward a productive dialogue with the scholar-teachers and practitioners of public administration who can give life to our ideas.

2 The Argument for Complementarity

EISENHOWER: *Thanks for coming to see me, Hector. I wanted to talk with you because the issues you raised in your letter are too important to leave to such brief statements. Please sit down.*

HECTOR: *I'm honored by the opportunity to explain myself more clearly, Mr. President.*

EISENHOWER: *Hector, it seems you don't think that independent agencies are any good at all for making public policy.*

HECTOR: *That's not quite right, sir. I frankly don't think that independent agencies are good for our representative government. They don't make it possible for you and Congress – the people Americans elected to represent them – to regulate important elements of our economic and social system in a comprehensive and efficient way. For me, that means, that they don't work.*

EISENHOWER: *But, come on, Hector, you know that efficiency wasn't what the founders of this great country had in mind when they designed a system that leaves me fighting tooth and nail with the powers that be in the Congress – and for every policy I promised the voters I'd try to put into practice. And I'm not even talking about the states!*

HECTOR: *Of course not, Mr. President.*

EISENHOWER: *Look, that's not the only problem with what you wrote. You seem to think that I should govern like a king, that I should have the capability to solve the nation's problems in a comprehensive way. I'll admit that would be nice sometimes, but that's sure as Sunday not what the Constitution gives me the power to do.*

HECTOR: *So, what are we supposed to do at the CAB, then? We can't keep our eyes on a unified objective, and Congress has left us untethered from your aims and easy meat for the very interests in the economy we are supposed to regulate.*

EISENHOWER: *Those are problems, sure they are, but you aren't seeing the bigger picture. In this government, sometimes, we have to give up the idea that we can solve every problem in order to* make sure that everyone can have a say in what we decide to do. Yes, those business interests you are thinking about are powerful because they're rich and they're focused on something clear, but I can't make a policy that ignores their concerns – especially if it hurts their investors and employees in some way – and neither can the CAB. What you seem to think of as inefficiency is really just democracy, Hector.

HECTOR: But, Mr. President, Congress can make an agency that isn't independent, and all I am saying is that if we want to make good national transportation policy, I think it needs to give you more authority.

EISENHOWER: That's a flattering and lawyerly answer, but it misses the mark when it comes to what our democracy really means. Sometimes, we can't have what you call "good" policy – and I think you mean comprehensive and coordinated – because we have to bring all of the interests of the people in this country to the table. When your colleagues are too influenced by the airlines, they're just not acting responsibly and that doesn't have one whit to do with the "independence" of the CAB – that's no structural problem, Hector – it's commissioners not understanding their role in our government.

HECTOR: Well, I certainly didn't mean to say that the structure of the CAB is a justification for commissioners to forget about democracy in this country, Mr. President.

EISENHOWER: I'm very sure you didn't, Hector. It is your responsibility – and mine, too – never to forget it. We do our jobs in the name of, on behalf of the people of this country. You are right that the Congress could have delegated to a civil aviation regulator that isn't independent, but it didn't, and when it comes to your responsibility to democracy, you can't pass the buck because you believe that democracy is harder to maintain in an independent commission. You just have to find a way to get it right.

The basic idea underlying the complementarity principle is almost deceptively plain: "Governance values ought to complement political values" (Bertelli 2021, 197). That is, the values of a political system should be reinforced by the practices enacted in *its* governance structures. Our emphasis in the last sentence is important. The complementarity principle applies to each political system and that set of governance structures that serve that system independently. Moreover, while Bertelli (2021) limits the scope of his argument to representative government and Heath (2020) focuses a compatible argument on liberal democracy, our intent is to generalize the argument to all varieties of government.[2] Pre-Rawls constitutions like that of the United States do not explicitly articulate long lists of rights and freedoms that ought to be part of their liberal democracies.[3] Value-congruity in one political system may emphasize different contours of democracy than it does in another system.

To begin to see why the complementarity principle is a requirement for public administration, consider two essential features of a well-functioning government: stability and sovereignty. In order for the members of a polity to function in their day-to-day lives, they need assurances that the fabric of society is and shall remain intact. A sovereign, self-governing state is necessary to maintain the integrity of the social fabric. In this way, the stability of the state relates to the stability of society. When governance structures reinforce the values of the political system of which they are a part, they both safeguard state sovereignty by discouraging seditious acts and contribute to social stability by positively promoting the sovereign will of the self-governing people.

The idea at the heart of the complementarity principle, that the political values of a state ought to be reinforced by its administrators, might strike some readers as obvious. We agree. But we also believe there is value in plainly stating the obvious, or in bringing the obvious into sharper relief. It is often the most obvious features of our shared reality that are the hardest to see or to keep in focus. Our contention is that a collective failure to keep value-congruity in focus in governance structure design has hindered our progress toward realizing certain political ideals, and that making this principle explicit – and, of course, putting it to use – can alleviate one major source of stagnation.

Bertelli's (2021) primary concern is with what the complementarity principle can do for representative governments. Thus, the relevant instantiation of the general form of the complementarity principle articulated above says: The values of a representative democracy should be reinforced by the practices of its elected representatives and its public administrators. Both representatives and public administrators under representative democratic regimes are public servants – they carry out the popularly elected policy agenda. We will call the efforts of public administrators to implement the legislated policy agenda policy

---

[2] Heath's (2020) argument is an instantiation of our more general argument. He essentially prescribes a professional ethic for a liberal democratic civil service wherein the principles of liberalism are those that ought to constrain policy workers' legitimate professional activities, and thus are the principles that ought to be reflected in institutions and governance structure design.

[3] John Rawls's *A Theory of Justice* was published in 1971.

work and those who make them policy workers (Bertelli 2016; 2021, 6). We do this to emphasize that policy workers make policy as they implement it through the choices within their discretion, and that they do not necessarily work directly for the government.[4] Policy workers, thus, enact (carry out) policies, and to enact with fidelity is to enact what was in fact chosen by the public will and to do so "in the name of all" (Cordelli 2020, 158).[5] Policy workers may be bureaucrats, but also private contractors, third-sector service providers and even coproducing citizens. Adhering to the complementarity principle forecloses the possibility of undermining democracy from within the state.

2.1 Responsibility

The word responsibility has three common meanings, all of which are important for understanding how policy work ought to be done. *Having* responsibility for something implies a duty to do it. *Taking* responsibility for something implies having the discretion to do it with more or less independence from other agents. *Being* responsible for something implies being held accountable to someone or to some collective for doing it.

Bertelli (2021, 197) argues that responsible policy work in a representative democracy must meet the following three criteria:

1. "A policy worker, when performing policy work, has an individual duty to reinforce political values through governance values."
2. "Policy workers cannot perform ultra vires policy work (i.e., that which is beyond their legal powers), even if it reinforces values."
3. "Policy workers *must* act to reinforce values if they have the capability to use means that are in fact likely to succeed in reinforcement. They are *positively obligated* to reinforce political values whenever possible and not ultra vires."

---

[4] Bertelli (2016, 225) emphasizes three important features of policy work: "(a) the effort performed by individuals (or groups of individuals); (b) the effort cannot easily be subdivided into tasks; and (c) the effort is connected with public policies . . . ." As a consequence, both National Security Agency contractor Edward Snowden and a host at a restaurant required by law to check specific documentation of COVID-19 vaccination are policy workers.

[5] Cordelli argues that as a matter of justice, "[it] is not enough that a properly authorized government determines and secures equal rights for all. It also matters that it does so 'in everyone's name,'" because (a) duties must be discharged by those who owe them or by a party who has standing to do so in the name of those who owe them, and (b) because "presumptively authoritative rules" that apply to everyone but are made with only a particular group of people in mind undermine the autonomy, the independence, and the wills of those outside of that group who are nevertheless subject to the rules in question (65). That representatives speak in everyone's name – that is, in the name of their entire constituency – reinforces the democratic value of the collective (or, as Cordelli conveys it, "omnilateral") will (65).

It is important to recognize that the responsibility of policy workers has an important implication for those who design governance structures, be they academics, advocates, or policymakers. Their designs ought to adhere to the complementarity principle. This is because well-designed governance structures are those which respect and facilitate the obligation of policy workers to behave responsibly, and that is both to refrain from acting outside of their purview and to reinforce, whenever possible, the values of their political systems through their individual positive actions. This is not yet the argument in favor of the indispensability of the complementarity principle, but rather the substantive view of responsible policy work that supports that positive argument, which we shall defend in due course. For our current purposes of formulating the argument, it is enough to state the criteria plainly.

2.2 The Formal Argument for Value-Congruity

Given the central idea underlying the complementarity principle, its basic formulations, and the substantive view of responsible policy work articulated above, we can formalize an argument in support of the complementarity principle as follows:

1. Responsible policy work requires policy workers to reinforce the political values of the system in which they operate.
2. Since responsible policy work requires policy workers to reinforce the political values of the system in which they operate, governance structures ought to be designed with the relevant political values and their reinforcement in mind.
3. The complementarity principle directs institutional designers to create governance structures with the relevant political values and their reinforcement in mind.
4. Thus, governance structure designers ought to adhere to the complementarity principle.

Value-congruity is essential to democracy, we contend, because the responsible conduct of policy work is essential to democratic governance. Governance structures that work against responsible policy work do not facilitate democratic self-rule. Notice that, at its core, responsible policy work as we have described it concerns normative judgments – normative *discretion* – and provides a substantive view about the legitimate sources of the values that guide discretionary judgments.

2.3 The Problem of Inductive Normative Reasoning

A common practical problem for which we believe the complementarity principle offers a much-needed remedy arises because of everyday contingencies in policy work. Policy workers regularly meet with circumstances in which they must use their discretion – sometimes their technical discretion, but often their *normative* discretion as well – in order to execute the functions of their positions.[6] In theorizing about "good" public administration, it is often suggested that we should look to the kinds of institutional designs and discretionary actions that have yielded favorable outcomes and extrapolate from those examples general guidance about the appropriate way to design administrative systems, including the scope of and constraints on administrative discretion. This is an ordinary process of inductive reasoning, but it presents us with a perennial problem: It is impossible to determine (with certainty) a general principle on the sole basis of observed patterns. Doing so is especially problematic when the "sample size" for those patterns is very small.

In the domain of public administration, we observe a tendency to reason from what has been demonstrably effective for one or a few agencies to some general principle that purportedly describes what it means to do "good public administration." With respect to administrative discretion, this kind of reasoning has led to a false choice between two positions. On one hand is the position that policy workers should be free to exercise their own normative discretion at will; on the other is the view that normative judgments are off limits to rank-and-file policy workers, and their discretion is limited only to technical aspects of policy implementation. But we know that it is a mistake to infer general principles from limited data, and governance structures designed to reflect either of these positions on authorized professional discretion are not likely to produce responsible policy work. A handful of instances, often taking place under idiosyncratic circumstances, where normative decisions made at the sole discretion of policy workers produced "good" results does not imply that a general policy or practice of freely wielded normative judgments will also "work" or "add value" across any given context. Nor do instances of institutional failure precipitated by policy workers' normative judgments imply that all normative discretion should be out of bounds.

The issue is one of filling in the general premise needed to validly reach a general conclusion on the basis of restricted or localized evidence. The evidence in question may seem reliable, but nevertheless its general applicability is likely inconclusive. To see this, consider the following number sequence puzzle:

1
11
21
<u>?</u>

---

[6] Bernardo Zacka (2017) discusses this issue in detail in the first chapter of his book, *When the State Meets the Street: Public Service and Moral Agency* (Belknap Press).

How should we fill in the unknown quantity? What number should come next in this sequence?

A reader may be thinking that 31 looks like a good candidate, because it seems to fit the probable operating principle generating the pattern observed thus far: 1+10 is 11; 11+10 is 21; 21+10 is 31; and so on. This infers the rule from the pattern by inductive reasoning rather than deducing the next number in the sequence by applying a known or specified rule. In fact, the next number in the sequence is 1211. The number after that is 111221. The reader has no way of knowing this and little chance of guessing it. The piece of information missing, which is crucial to accurately predicting the next number in the sequence, is the rule governing the generation of the sequence. This sequence (known as the Conway sequence) is self-describing; it is a "see-and-say" sequence.[7]

1
11 (One 1)
21 (Two 1s)
1211 (One 2, one 1)
111221 (One 1, one 2, two 1s)
And so on.

Once you know the rule, you can deduce from that rule and the pattern you see what the next number in the sequence will be. The problem in real life is that there are few instances in which we actually know the rule. Since in many domains of human life, all we have are observations, we are often forced to make our best approximations of underlying organizing principles as we go along. Our best option is to infer a general principle from what we in fact observe. That is how scientific reasoning proceeds and how we make scientific progress. There is no reason, though, that determinations of what constitutes *good* public administration need to be based on this kind of reasoning. That is not a scientific question, but a normative one, and in the normative domain, one need not reason on an inductive basis alone.

General normative principles can be constructed by top-down processes beginning in conceptual analysis rather than by a bottom-up process that begins in observation. The complementarity principle is of the former variety, and it provides an alternative to inductive reasoning on normative matters in day-to-day policy work. We think that theorists are mistaken to default to inductive reasoning on normative questions about good policy work, and that the complementarity principle corrects that mistake by supplying a general rule which, if followed in

---

[7] We are indebted to Achille Varzi for this example, which he used in a public talk in Kansas City on the problem of induction (c. 2011).

governance structure design, should reliably facilitate good (i.e., responsible) public administration. It does this by building value-reinforcement mechanisms into the structures themselves and by providing general guidance for policy workers' everyday use of normative discretion. The hope is that rather than reasoning like Commissioner Hector did from his circumstances to the general conclusion that independent commissions should not be charged with making policy, people in Hector's position can look to the guiding principle and decide whether it would be responsible in these circumstances for an independent agency to be involved in policymaking.

2.4 Inductive Normative Reasoning in Public Administration

The complementarity principle is meant to supply an alternative to inductive normative reasoning in public administration, that is, the tendency to conclude that whatever works is what constitutes good policy work – that whatever gets the desired outcome is what makes a policy or its implementation good. We think that employing this kind of reasoning in the design and execution of governance arrangements, especially with respect to the permissibility of normative discretionary judgments, is a mistake that often leads to undemocratic practices and to irresponsible policy work.[8]

A wide variety of arguments about "good" policy work succumb to the problem of inductive normative reasoning. To take one example, Goodsell (2011) contends that policy work done within organizations with "mission mystique" can improve the work that is done and enhance the organization's link to democracy. He describes the "mission mystique agency" as one that "is endowed with an aura of positive institutional charisma that is derived from the nature of its mission and how well it is carried out" (477). Its benefit for "career employees" of the organization is that "the mystique fosters a personal commitment to advancement of the mission" and for "attentive outsiders, it generates admiration and respect" (477–478). He argues, inter alia, that mission mystique makes it possible for policy workers to maintain and build capacity even as representatives change the aims of policy work. His premises are observations like these: (a) The National Park Service has its "source of mystique" in "the magnificent beauty and deep cultural meaning of the national parks under their care" and (b) "[a]lthough its work has experienced varied treatment by presidential administrations since its creation under President Kennedy … its popularity on college campuses and fame around the world are as strong as

---

[8] It can also lead to bad outcomes even when it is intended to yield good ones. See Joyce and Cartwright (2020), arguing that education policy adopted from the What Works Clearinghouse on purportedly evidence-based grounds does not and indeed cannot reliably improve education policy or outcomes.

ever" (482). His conclusion is "to urge agencies to look to a *normative ideal* called mission mystique" so that they can shore up their "institutional center," which means a "clearly articulated and necessary mission; continuity of a competent workforce and institutional memory; and a generous and confident capacity for change" (490, emphasis added).

Another example is the value of a reputation for doing "good" policy work (Carpenter 2001; 2010). When an organization develops a reputation doing "good" policy work, say, protecting whistleblowers, that organization is seen by representatives as the right source of policy workers for protecting whistle-blowers, and this gives the organization lasting authority with both governments and key stakeholders. Bertelli and Busuioc (2021, 40) note that observations about reputation-enhancing authority become premises in an "epistemic view" of reputation: (a) "the preferences of elected politicians, whether or not they are induced by the wants of the electorate, will not (or have not) achieved a 'correct' policy," (b) reputation "over time and through experience with changing states of the world . . . bureaucrats to become better at making 'correct' policies, and they can use their reputation with audiences to maintain them," so (c) the policy workers should negotiate with, rather than be controlled by, elected representatives. The basis for the second point is the observation of evidence of it in agencies such as the Food and Drug Administration (Carpenter 2010) or the US Post Office (Carpenter 2001). Bertelli and Busuioc (2021) warn that this epistemic claim sets the stage for irresponsible policy work because a "good" reputation diminishes representatives' incentive to monitor policy work and allows policy workers to use claims to stakeholders as a way to pressure representatives to agree with their version of "good" policy work.

2.5 Defending the Complementarity Principle

We think that the complementarity principle supplies the general normative guidance necessary for agency designers to facilitate, and indeed for policy workers to identify and to do, "good" (i.e., responsible) policy work in any given context. The task of the rest of this essay is to put the meat on the bones of the argument, explicated in Section 2.2, for the indispensability of adherence to the complementarity principle in governance structure design. We proceed as follows.

Section 3 supports the first premise with reasons why meeting the criteria enumerated above constitutes responsible policy work. This discussion pieces together what exactly we mean by democracy and democratic values and ultimately roots out the values of representative democracy. It also specifies what we mean by "good" or "bad" governance. One notable outcome of the discussion in this section is the conclusion that adherence to the complementarity principle is *outcome independent*. Outcomes are not and cannot be the only things that matter. Adhering to complementarity when designing the means of public administration is positively prescribed even if it sometimes results in suboptimal end states.

Section 4 supports the second premise by addressing the problem of irresponsible policy work. That is, we discuss the consequences of governance structures that divert the policy workers laboring within them from responsibility. One such structure is the representative bureaucracy (Kingsley 1944; Mosher 1968), which is designed to improve outcomes according to an ambiguous criterion of social equity (see Frederickson 1990). We show that while the policy-worker-as-citizen can adhere to a vision of social equity, doing so on the job in a way that elides responsibility as defined above is not consistent with democracy.

In Section 5, we further support the second premise of our argument for the indispensability of the complementarity principle through an illustrative case that contrasts two different instantiations of a governance structure that Bertelli (2021, 110) calls representative agency, which allows groups of citizens "to facilitate collective decisions that legitimate subsequent policy work." The case illuminates the difference between a representative agency structure that reinforces the political values of representative democracy with one that (perhaps inadvertently) undermines them.

Section 6 offers support for the third premise in our argument by explaining the features of the complementarity principle in greater detail. We show that the principle is genuinely action-guiding and explicit in its purpose, that the kind of guidance it offers has up to now been lacking, and that without such guidance, institutional designers run the risk of wasting their time and energy designing what might turn out to be bad governance structures. That is, they will either fail to facilitate responsible policy work or, worse, positively encourage policy workers to act irresponsibly.

In Section 6, we summarize the argument and briefly recap the highlights in support of its premises. More importantly, we offer a few thoughts about how the complementarity principle can help to improve the democratic content of the governance structures we critique.

3 Responsible Policy Work

HECTOR: *I'm beginning to feel that you expect the CAB to do more than just make policy, Mr. President.*

EISENHOWER: *Nonsense, Hector. That's exactly what it needs to do, but it can't undermine our democracy in the process.*

HECTOR: *Yes, I understand that democracy obligates us to represent the people who are impacted by our policies.*

EISENHOWER: *But representing them isn't your responsibility – that's for me and the Congress. Your responsibility is to keep our democracy at the forefront of your mind as you work through all the information and arguments from all those who want a say in aviation policies. Your responsibility is to keep all the people in the mix, not just those with technical briefs and those with the loudest voices, to the best of your ability. Your responsibility is not to overstep your authority and do things that Congress didn't authorize you to do.*

HECTOR: *I understand the limits of our authority, Mr. President.*

EISENHOWER: *I have every confidence that you do, Hector. It's the difference between representing interests and considering the people that seems less clear to you. When your colleagues hear only the loudest voices, they ignore their responsibility to the people – to all the people.*

HECTOR: *You are a representative of all the people, and that's why I've been arguing that you should have more authority over the CAB.*

EISENHOWER: *You have to play the hand that Congress dealt you. The CAB is independent. I am not your shortcut unless Congress changes the law. No matter what, your process has to be consistent with your responsibility to the people.*

HECTOR: *This is harder than I thought, Mr. President.*

EISENHOWER: *I've had to learn this job, too, Hector.*

We begin our defense of the complementarity principle by focusing on the first premise of the argument sketched in Section 2.2. That is, we argue for the democratic importance of responsible policy work. To defend this view, we must do several things. First, we need to situate the argument within a particular political framework. Second, we must articulate what we take to be the values of that political framework and why. Once these two components are on the table, we can address each criterion of responsible policy work in turn, offering a full explanation as to why each is necessary. Third, we defend the claim that a policy worker acts responsibly by adhering to an individual duty to reinforce political values through governance values when performing policy work. Fourth, we justify the criterion of responsibility requiring that policy workers may not act ultra vires in doing policy work, even if such action reinforces political values. Fifth, we defend the final criterion, namely that responsible policy workers are positively obligated to reinforce political values when they have the capability to do so. Finally, we defend the claim that the foregoing criteria in concert are jointly sufficient for responsible policy work. In so doing, we draw out two essential puzzles of responsibility in public administration: the problem of roles and the problem of levels.

3.1 Democracy and Representative Government

Let us begin, then, by articulating a broad conception of democracy and the values it embodies. To fully situate the argument, we reiterate that Bertelli's (2021) project is concerned with what the complementarity principle can do for governance structure design in representative democracies. With this scope restriction, his intention is to address the majority of operating democracies in the current global landscape; it is not to imply that complementarity is only applicable within such states. On the contrary, and as we shall argue toward the end of this section, the principle applies regardless of the form a government takes. Representative government is both widespread and largely taken to be among the best forms of government available from the perspective of human freedom, and it has flourished. It is also the form of government under which most of our likely readership lives. Its supremacy is not, however, a foregone conclusion for the purposes of this argument. Under any form of government, responsible policy work must meet the criteria specified above, but our primary defense of those criteria will be articulated from within the framework of representative democratic government.

Democratic values are found in the very notion of democracy. Democracy's bumper-sticker slogan reads: government of the people, by the people, and for the people. As with any system of government, it organizes a society, and oversees a populace. Its governing members count themselves as numbers among that populace, serving and governing themselves in the same manner that they serve and govern the rest of the population (Hobbes 1668 ; Locke 1689; Rousseau 2019). They serve and govern in accordance with a legal code (Dworkin 1990; Hart 1961; Raz 2009). Those living in a democratic society are free to live their lives as they see fit within the bounds of the law, and to pursue their own ends in order to build fulfilling lives (Rawls 1999; Raz 1986). Essentially, members of a democratic society must be afforded equal voice as well as equal rights and liberties, and they must be able to lead autonomous lives. These are the fundamentals of democratic society, at least from an ideal perspective, and they yield a rich characterization of democracy:

> Democracy is a collaborative exercise in self-governance among the members of society who are guided by the rule of law, each of whom is entitled to voice his or her own preferences, to have an equal say in matters of public concern, and each of whom is entitled to enact his or her own conception of the good within reason, where within reason means that the exercise of one's own conception of the good does not fundamentally interfere with (i.e., does not wholesale impede and does not depend on significantly impeding) anyone else's exercise of the same.

From this description of democracy, we can begin to extract a preliminary list of democratic values. These include self-governance, self-representation on matters of public concern, free and equal participation in public decision-making processes, equal voice (i.e., each person's say matters equally), freedom of thought and action, and reasonable value pluralism. Left open are choices about how to organize a system of self-governance, how to conduct public decision-making processes, how to count or group constituent inputs, and what kinds of matters count as matters of public concern (among other things). For instance, a democratic system might rely on different kinds of input mechanisms and different methods of input aggregation, and it might rely on direct or indirect representation (see, e.g., Bertelli 2021, chs. 2–3).

3.2 Fidelitous Representation

Representative democracy has all the values of democracy in general – broad public participation, equal voice, collective will, and reasonable pluralism – plus the value of fidelitous representation, that is, the accurate representation of the collective will, which requires preserving the salience of any number of competing considerations. A representative represents with fidelity by taking into consideration the interests of not just those who voted for her, but all of those who reside within her district. In practice, constituencies are delineated along geographical, not ideological lines. Thus, to represent one's entire constituency with fidelity, a representative must take into consideration not only the victorious bid on any given matter of public concern, but also the relative weights of support between it and any competing bids, and the relative weights of support among the bids that did not prevail in addition to any socially relevant features that set backers of different bids apart from each other, and the relative importance of those bids to those constituent subgroups. Why? Because this is what is required to represent everyone in a pluralist society, valuing their inputs equally, enacting the public will while also respecting minority opinions. This kind of weighing and measuring, used in concert with an appropriate principle of distributive justice, gives us a formula with which to prioritize the various public matters at issue in any given place at any given time.

When we say that fidelitous representation is that which *accurately* represents the collective will, our notion of accuracy is pluralistic and democratic. Everyone's voice counts equally, everyone's interests count equally, and nobody's voice or interests are swept aside by virtue of being in the minority. Notice that this is not the same thing as impartial representation. To be truly impartial is to do more than leave out one's party affiliation in representative decision-making; it is, by definition, to leave out the kinds of considerations mentioned above. Moreover, fidelitous representation does not require one to leave one's political party affiliation at the door; it only requires that one's partisan zeal be appropriately tempered by the presence and interests of non-party members in one's constituency. Fidelitous representation, then, is not impartial, but, rather, embraces a kind of "weighted partiality." For instance, because certain career civil servants are likely to find themselves in positions that charge them with making policy decisions, the concept of fidelitous representation extends also to them in something like the Weberian civil service neutrality sense. But, here again, "neutrality" is not quite the right word, since using professional discretion in order to enact policies with fidelity may involve *personal* neutrality, but it does not necessitate full (or "true") neutrality among all competing interests, including partisan ones, the consideration of which may be relevant.

One way to achieve fidelitous representation is by bringing the *demos* into the process of policy work via representative agency structures, which is the focus of Section 4.4. Before we get into examples, though, it is worth considering why we ought to prefer a representative democratic system (if, in fact, we should) to something like direct democracy, which is imbued with fidelitous (because it is one-to-one) representation from the start.

Opting for a representative system of democratic government is not, as some have argued (e.g., Cordelli 2020), a non-defeatable, logical consequence of basic human dignity and reason.[9] It is a matter of practicality and pragmatism. Ideally, a fully democratic system would consider every individual person's will

---

[9] It is not clear that adopting a representative democratic system necessarily follows from facts about basic human dignity and reason as Cordelli claims it does. It may be true that these human characteristics offer strong support for the adoption of representative government, and perhaps stronger support for it than other available governance system, but it is possible that arguing for it the way that she does (as a logical consequence of basic facts about humanity) forecloses a lot more than privatization. Although our space here is too limited to take it up in detail, the issue is worth revisiting in the future.

on every separate matter of public concern. But one-to-one representation (that is, *self*-representation) tends only to work on a small scale with a population made up entirely of able-minded adults. There is strength in numbers. There are many other good reasons to band together as a unified polity under largely shared political values. Individual voices get lost and muddled in vast seas of other voices, so as a matter of practicality, in large and largely pluralistic polities, representative government is the next best option. It pares down the number of voices at play, but it is intentionally designed such that representatives act as conduits for their constituencies, bundling the interests and individual wills of the people they represent, and expressing and advocating for these to the best of their abilities. It also provides a mechanism for distilling myriad positions on individual issues into broad policy platforms which reduces the number of options from which voters must choose, and which thereby combats indecision. A voter need not assent to every policy position in a political platform to prefer it over its rivals. And besides, it is easier to exercise influence over individual policy positions one does not expressly endorse from a vantage point within a party or a friendly constituency than it is from without.

As we shall argue shortly, responsible policy work flows from fidelitous representation, which is itself an instance, and an expression, of value-congruity. If a type of policy work is duly authorized through fidelitous representation, it would be utterly revolutionary for policy workers to act beyond their legal discretion when doing it. This would allow a policy worker to thwart the efforts of representatives to make democracy work. Of course, policy workers may well believe that any of the democratic values we have discussed above are not being upheld in policy work, and if they have the legal authority to maintain those values, responsibility dictates that policy workers are individually obligated to do so. We offer much more detail on these points in Section 3.3, but flagging them here helps to clarify the trajectory of the argument.

Before moving on, it is worth taking stock of the argument up to this point. In this section, we have so far offered an idealized characterization of representative democracy and a list of values that responsible policy workers in representative democratic systems are duty-bound to uphold. As indicated above, we will flesh out and defend the criteria of responsible policy work articulated in Section 2.1, but first, we should address a probable objection to our defense so far.

3.3 The Problem of Roles

One might object at this point that while complementarity is beginning to seem like a good principle for governance structure design in a representative democracy, adherence to the complementarity principle within any system of government means reinforcing the values of bad governments (the kind that systematically violate human rights, for instance) as well as good ones. Creating this kind of reinforcing feedback decreases the odds of dismantling and replacing bad governmental systems with good ones (those more conducive to human flourishing).

We consider this objection constructive insofar as it helps to clarify one of the primary features of the principle. The complementarity principle applies only to those who are concerned with designing governance structures that are supposed to be effective within a particular political framework. Just as the concept of democracy is silent on the desirability of particular political institutions, the complementarity principle is silent on the desirability of any given political system. Its purpose is to facilitate – or at least not to preclude – responsible policy work on the part of everyday policy workers. This is, in part, a matter of basic social stability. Policy workers carry out the everyday governmental operations that enable society to function. Doing responsible policy work enables it to function under conditions of stability. As we mentioned briefly above, stability is one of the primary reasons for forming a government. Social stability is essential to basic human flourishing. It is the foundation on which one can build a life, cultivate an identity, start and raise a family, embark on and build a career, and so on. And this is true under any kind of regime. Even if one's options are severely restricted under an oppressive government, the expectation that things will remain as they are and that the basic structure of society is not likely to radically change overnight is essential to building a life for oneself in one's present circumstances. Those circumstances cannot be vulnerable to serious upheaval, which adherence to complementarity guards against.

This does mean that governance structures designed to operate in an authoritarian state should be designed such that day-to-day policy work reinforces the values of that authoritarian system. Authoritarianism may be a suboptimal state of affairs, but rogue policy workers carrying out their work within such a state, enacting policies in ways that complement, say, socialist values instead of the ones embedded in their own governmental system, will not magically create more optimal conditions. Deviating from authoritarian norms in such a way is unlikely to make anyone's life easier or to instill socialist values in the government. In fact, it is far more likely only to make the administration of public services less efficient, less stable, and less effective. Heeding the complementarity principle ensures that the operating government, however "bad" it may be, will at least keep serving the public in whatever ways it does so. Might worsening socio-economic conditions accelerate public agitation for change? Maybe, but to do so would nevertheless be a revolutionary, unilateral, unauthorized move (by either authoritarian or socialist standards), and an abuse of the policy worker's position within the government. In short, it would be *irrespon-sible*. It is irresponsible to knowingly and intentionally mobilize what government machinery is under one's own control against the values of the system, and in so doing, to jeopardize the stability of people's social environments in the service of one's own values.

Moreover, to behave in such a revolutionary way is to make the perhaps inaccurate assumption that all people in fact would prefer not to live under an authoritarian regime. It assumes what constitutes "good" government in substantive terms. The complementarity principle assumes nothing about "good" government in that sense. Its operating notion of goodness is purely functional. This government is "good" insofar as it is functioning optimally according to its own principles, whatever those may be. We remain agnostic as to the substance of good government because we respect the fact that reasonable people disagree on how best to fill in the details, and our aim is to supply a general principle that anyone designing governance mechanisms in any system can use to positive effect. Hobbes argued that imbuing a single ruler with the power to make governmental decisions for the people was the only way to secure "good" social order. Rousseau believed social order could best be achieved through governance systems that reflect the unified, collective will of the people, as established by majority rule. Whatever the details, though, the complementarity principle applies.

Substantive applications of the complementarity principle assess the goodness of government according to whether or not the government is functioning in accordance with a particular set of political values. Heath (2020), for instance, argues that public administration ought to be guided by the values of liberalism. His argument is essentially a special case of the more general argument we make here. Heath argues for value complementarity between the substantive values of the political system and the norms that ought to guide public policy work within a specifically liberal democratic framework. He argues that in a liberal democracy, the values of liberalism (and not those of democracy more generally) are those that ought to guide the administration of public goods and services because liberal values more comprehensively capture the values of the system. That is, specifically liberal values, because they are more comprehensive, are more practically applicable than general, perhaps somewhat abstract or obscure democratic values. Therefore, hewing closely to them as practical guides will yield better outcomes for people living in liberal democratic regimes. The same line of argument is available to people who believe that authoritarian rule is desirable.

While adherence to the complementarity principle means designing governance structures that are meant to function in authoritarian or despotic regimes to reinforce the values of authoritarianism or despotism, it does not foreclose the possibility of sociopolitical change. The crucial point is that it is not the place of policy workers to undermine the sovereignty or jeopardize the stability of the governments they serve. To do that is to do irresponsible policy work. Things may not be going well for the *demos* under authoritarian rule. Nevertheless, consider how much worse things could be for the people if policy workers were to follow institutional designs that (intentionally or otherwise) gummed up the works of the public administration they do have. Radical political change ought not to be led or carried out by the bureaucracy.

This is also not to say that policy workers must acquiesce or submit to an unjust or otherwise bad governmental structure outside of their formal roles as policy workers. A person is a person, and a policy worker qua person has the freedom to express discontent, to agitate for change, to vote as she sees fit, and to pursue her own conception of the good just as any other person does. This distinction between a policy worker qua policy worker and a policy worker qua person (or civilian, or citizen, or community member) draws out the first of two problems we take to be at issue with respect to responsible policy work. We call this the *problem of roles:*

> What one may permissibly do in the interest of justice or fairness (or any other value) in one's official capacity is and ought to be constrained by both the spirit and the letter of the law, *and* by the values of the system within which one carries out one's duties. What the same person may permissibly do in the interest of justice or fairness (and so forth) in her capacity as a civilian or member of society *simpliciter* is and ought not to be so constrained.

We shall have more to say about this problem (and its resolution under the complementarity principle) shortly, but for now our point is that it is preferable to have policy workers behaving responsibly even if that means reinforcing bad political values, if only for the sake of having things go as well as can be expected given the circumstances. To see what makes this the clearly preferable state of affairs, consider what conditions might be like in any given society if all it took to fatally undermine a government's individual initiatives, its overarching policy agenda, or indeed its sovereignty was going straight to its rank-and-file policy workers and marshaling their actions against the very system of which they are a part in a campaign to completely change the political landscape. Such a system would be vulnerable not only to the whims of policy workers themselves, but also to outside influence – even coercion – by more powerful forces than any directly targeted policy worker could reasonably be expected to resist. Designing governance structures in ways that take seriously and, in a sense, "bake in" responsible policy work (i.e., policy work that reinforces the political values of the system) guards against such corrupting influences, which itself remains a good feature even if those corrupting influences might keep the society in question from coming closer to realizing democratic ideals.

While the problem of roles is not unknown among public administration scholars, its democratic implications are less carefully charted. Consider cases of "guerrilla government" as explored by O'Leary (2010, 8), which is constituted of "actions of career public servants who work against the wishes – either implicitly or explicitly communicated – of their superiors." She sees this as "a form of dissent that is usually carried out by those who are dissatisfied" with the policy work in which they are involved, though "for strategic reasons" these guerrillas "choose not to go public with their concerns" with only a few "outing themselves as whistle-blowers" (8). This is a clear instance of the problem of roles, and the guerrillas seem well aware of this: Guerrillas "work on the assumption that their work outside their agencies provides them a latitude that is not available in formal settings" (9). Their discretionary action is unguided. To wit, "[m]ost have a wider conceptualization of their work than that articulated by their agency's formal and informal statements of mission" and some guerrillas are less guided still, "more freewheeling, doing what feels right to them" (9). Guerrillas irresponsibly resolve the problem of roles precisely because they "bring the credibility of the formal, bureaucratic, political system with them, as well as the credibility of their individual professions" to lend legitimacy to their positions.

O'Leary (2010, 9) recognizes the essence of the problem of roles, namely that "guerrillas run the risk of being unregulated themselves" and that they may be "promoting policies that may not be compatible with the system as a whole." Still, the democratic importance of responsible policy work is not fully recognized in her conclusions. In making them, O'Leary (2010, 16) defines "ethical decision making" by quoting Cooper (1998, 256–257), who claimed, "[a] truly responsible administrator will bear an obligation to propose changes when they become problematic for the wishes of the public, inconsistent with professional judgment, or in conflict with personal conscience." We believe that Cooper's statement resolves the problem of roles and the problem of levels (to be articulated in Section 4.2) in an irresponsible way because it identifies the wrong object of responsibility. Policy workers are responsible to the *demos* and the boundaries of responsible action are demarcated by the values of the system they serve and the law. Representatives are obligated to represent the same people with fidelity, raising what we will soon call the problem of levels, and policy workers cannot undermine that representation because their moral compass points them elsewhere without irresponsibly addressing the problem of roles. Crucially, we contend that policy workers in democratic regimes are obligated to act to reinforce democratic values if it is possible to do so and if the action likely to succeed in reinforcing those values. They are not obligated to act because of their own "conscience" or because their profession would encourage such action. Conscience and profession are valid reasons to "propose changes" just as they are valid reasons to resign one's position as a policy worker. They are not criteria for responsible action. We will take up this matter in greater detail momentarily.

To see the problem of roles in the context of a representative democracy and how this problem might be alleviated by adhering to the complementarity principle, consider the contrasts between the cases of Edward Snowden and Cassidy Hutchinson. Snowden, acting in his capacity as a concerned citizen, believed himself to be upholding democratic values in exposing potentially explosive classified information to multiple entities, including journalists and foreign government agents.[10] Hutchinson also acted in her capacity as a concerned citizen in testifying before Congress about sensitive and potentially explosive information regarding the prior knowledge and states of mind of top government officials whose actions on and leading up to the events at the Capitol on January 6, 2021, may have jeopardized the stability of the United States government, and did in fact compromise the immediate safety of myriad representatives, officials, and civilians.

Many see Snowden as a hero: He exposed the government surveillance of ordinary citizens on a massive scale, at great risk to himself, for the benefit of us all. Others see him as a criminal: He stole government secrets and disclosed them without regard to the ways in which doing so might jeopardize national security. In his capacity as a policy worker, a contractor with the National Security Agency (NSA), he acted irresponsibly. In his capacity as a citizen and a member of the affected community, his behavior seems warranted. His position was not enviable. A serious tension developed for him between his obligations as dictated by his role as a policy worker and his obligations as befitting his values as a citizen. Note, though, that he only had the capacity to act as he did as a citizen because of his role as a policy worker. He only had access to the information he did because of the security clearance he was granted by the NSA, and he was, in his official capacity, sworn to respect the secrecy of sensitive and classified government information. Importantly, in his role as a policy worker, he was not forced to behave irresponsibly. He was not con-strained in such a way that he had no choice but to behave irresponsibly to achieve his purported goals as a concerned citizen.

---

[10] We thank Andrew Williams for suggesting that we explore this problem.

Snowden considered himself to be a textbook whistleblower. He exposed waste and inefficiency (extensive governmental resources being used to secure miniscule intelligence advantages), serious abuses of power (the unwarranted invasion of citizens' privacy by their government on a massive, national scale), and gross mismanagement with respect to data handling by the NSA. Questions about how he went about exposing these problems, why he felt justified, and why he went about it the way he did bring his status as a whistleblower into question. Whistleblowing is protected because it offers policy workers a way to reinforce democratic values responsibly by disclosing waste, fraud, abuse and so forth in an appropriately controlled environment.

According to Snowden's own version of events, he first raised his concerns somewhat informally with colleagues, asking how they thought the public would react to these programs if they were exposed and explained on the front page of the newspaper. He said that colleagues agreed that the public's reaction would be overwhelmingly negative. He said that he brought these concerns to his direct supervisors (a claim which those supervisors dispute), and that he formally raised the issue several times through the appropriate channels that were available to him.[11] Feeling as though his concerns had been dismissed, he proceeded to steal classified information and subsequently to disclose the classified materials he had taken to journalists and foreign government agents. Included in those materials were details about how the agency went about gathering the information it did, the disclosure of which he argued was necessary to prove his claims. In disclosing these details, he exposed state secrets, and probably cutting-edge intelligence-gathering methods and technologies to potentially hostile foreign entities.

According to our criteria, Snowden acted irresponsibly. Confronting the problem of roles, he was torn between upholding his values as an everyday citizen of the United States and his duties as an NSA contractor. Had the NSA structure been designed in accordance with the complementarity principle, Snowden's dilemma might have been easier to resolve without resorting to taking professionally irresponsible action. If the agency was designed with democratic value reinforcement in mind, he might have had better guidance as to how he could uphold his obligation to act responsibly in his capacity as an NSA contractor. Snowden's is a particularly illuminating case because the various factors at play within it (a) explain why his professional obligations deserved to be given priority over his personal values, (b) illustrate the importance of value complementarity in policy work more generally, and

---

[11] The NSA Office of General Council acknowledges receipt of one email from Snowden "raising policy and legal questions" with respect to the surveillance programs in question (*NBC News* 2014).

(c) demonstrate the salience of fidelitous representation. Moreover, his case shows how all of this holds true even when the government in question is behaving badly.

Snowden expressly believed that he was acting in accordance with democratic values. He rightly thought that, upon learning what he knew about the surveillance programs being used to collect their data, their personal correspondence, and their personal information, the people of the United States would consider the NSA program to be a gross invasion of privacy in violation of their constitutional rights against unlawful searches and seizures. The first problem for responsibility was that Snowden acted ultra vires. He acted in defiance of both the letter and the spirit of the law. He has correctly pointed out that he was not protected under federal whistleblower protection laws at the time of his disclosures. Had he disclosed the NSA's programs and the corroborating documentation he procured to, say, a member of Congress with the proper security clearance to review that classified information, he would have been subject to arrest and prosecution. Though he would not have been formally protected as a contractor, it would have been reasonable to disclose his information according to procedures open to regular NSA employees and to demand the same kind of protection that any such employee would be afforded. Moreover, the responsible thing for his colleagues employed directly at NSA to do would have been to take his concerns to the appropriate entities *for* him, since doing so would reinforce the political values of the system of which they are a part, since they could do so without acting ultra vires, and since they (unlike Snowden) had the capability to do so using means within their legal constraints that would likely succeed in reinforcement.

It would have been equally reasonable for those to whom Snowden might have disclosed to act in their official capacity to uphold democratic values by doing whatever it took to provide him with the same protection his colleagues would have had. Members of Congress could have introduced a whistleblower protection bill to cover his actions, NSA officials could have defended his actions in court because that would square with the spirit of the law. However, such disclosure, to be responsible, also would have required that Snowden could count on those to whom he disclosed the information to respond appropriately, that is, with fidelity to the public interest, to his interests as a whistleblower, and to the democratic values that Snowden was trying to maintain. We cannot emphasize this enough. Snowden did not feel as though he could count on that kind of treatment, so instead, in the second problem for responsibility, he absconded with the information and disclosed it in spectacularly irresponsible fashion to reporters and foreign government agents. This reportedly damaged American intelligence gathering capabilities worldwide and potentially jeopardized the stability of the United States by unilaterally undermining the people's trust in their government and in their elected representatives.

Having bypassed the channels deemed appropriate by, at least, the spirit of whistleblower protection laws, Snowden bypassed the people's elected representatives, effectively denying them the opportunity to represent with fidelity – that is, to act in their constituents' interests to stop the program of mass surveillance being conducted against them by their own government agencies. Because existing whistleblower protection laws and the democratic values underwriting them would have protected any regular NSA employee, there were obvious channels open to Snowden to be able to responsibly disclose the waste, abuse, and mismanagement he had identified. The problem lies in the structure of his policy work. Without the appropriate value reinforcement mechanisms built into the NSA organization and its contracts, particularly whistleblower protection for those with high-level security clearance, and without the assurance that his disclosure would be handled with fidelity by those to whom he ought to have disclosed, Snowden felt obligated to both expose the agency's abuses and to protect himself through irresponsible actions, specifically those that violate the second criterion for responsible policy work.

Hutchinson's case is slightly different, but it illustrates how it is possible to navigate the problem of roles in the wake of a government behaving badly without violating either personal values or professional obligations. Hutchinson recently defied her former boss and the former President of the United States by testifying before the Select Committee to Investigate the January 6 Attack on the United States Capitol, disclosing personal conversations between top advisors to President Trump along with details about the states of mind of the President and other actors as well as their behavior leading up to and on January 6, 2021. In her capacity as assistant to the White House Chief of Staff, Hutchinson had a duty to keep the confidence of West Wing officials while reinforcing the values of representative democracy to the best of her ability and where possible. As a citizen, she wanted the American people to know what she knew about the thoughts and actions of key officials in the days and hours before an attempt to stop the transfer of presidential power.[12]

As policy workers, both Snowden and Hutchinson had an individual duty to reinforce the political values of the system in which they operated, to do so within the law, and to act on that duty if likely to succeed in reinforcing the relevant values. Both acted at great personal risk. One of them behaved

---

[12] Notably, Hutchinson made this distinction in her testimony, first expressing her assessment of the situation in her official capacity as assistant to the White House Chief of Staff and then expressing her assessment of it as a concerned citizen.

responsibly and the other did not. In the absence of governance structures designed with value complementarity in mind, getting it right can come down to the toss of a coin. Though Hutchinson maintained confidence until she could offer testimony to an appropriate authority, she might just as well have reached out to any number of reputable journalists covering the story. Her actions have given elected representatives the opportunity to represent their constituents with fidelity, which reinforce the democratic values at the heart of the electoral process and the democratic value of fidelitous representation. That outcome was not preordained. The governance structure within which she was operating did not facilitate, much less ensure, responsible action. But the congressional committee did. In speaking to it, and through it, to the nation, she upheld her individual duty to take actions that were likely to reinforce the political values of representative democracy, where she could do so within the bounds of the spirit and the letter of the laws than constrain her in her official capacity. Snowden did not.

Designing institutions in accordance with the complementarity principle positions policy workers for success in their efforts to look out for the good of the people. The structures of public administration should be designed to facilitate responsible policy work – work that reinforces the political values of representative democracy. But why, one might ask, should I believe that these specific criteria are and ought to be the criteria for responsible policy work?

3.4 Components of Responsible Policy Work

At long last, the ground has been sufficiently cleared for us to flesh out and to defend the three criteria of responsible policy work articulated in Section 2.1. The first criterion Bertelli (2021, 197) gives for responsible policy work is that "a policy worker, when performing policy work, has an individual duty to reinforce political values through governance values." Call this the *individual duty* component of responsibility. In a representative democracy, the individual duty component of responsible policy work holds because one's role as a policy worker in the larger political system is that of a policy worker who is meant to carry out or to enact the policies that have been chosen by the public through an official electoral process. In other words, it is one's job as a policy worker to function not as an individual with her own will, but as a component part of the machinery of the governmental system of which she is a part – this, simply put, is the functional explanation of what a policy worker does in a representative democracy. Because a policy worker's role is to function as a part of the system rather than as an individual, value reinforcement is an intrinsic feature of "good" policy work in the same way that teeth meeting their counterparts in order to turn gears and belts using friction to spin plates makes them good parts of a machine, as opposed to defective or broken ones.[13]

Importantly, this explanation of what it is to be a policy worker does not foreclose the use of authorized normative discretion in policy enactment. Just as an algorithm uses hypotheticals in logic gates to choose a proper course of action, policy workers have different avenues available to them, any of which, if followed with fidelity, might constitute a responsible execution of the function in question. The key to using one's authorized normative discretion responsibly is reasoning according to the right set of values – the values of the system one serves.

All of these criteria, including the *individual duty* criterion, follow from the concept of government, or what it means to govern. Having opted for a particular system of government is to have opted for a particular set of political values – the set of political values according to which the system shall operate. As a component of that system, a policy worker is bound by the same set of political values – the values by which the system operates. Her personal values do not and ought not to enter into contention when she is deciding how she should execute her function in her official capacity. For all intents and purposes, while she is serving in her official capacity, her values are the values of the system. The *individual duty* component of responsibility, then, delimits which values may and may not enter into the deliberative processes of persons engaged in responsible policy work.

The second criterion says that "policy workers cannot perform ultra vires policy work, even if it reinforces values" (Bertelli 2021), because to do so is to act beyond the constraints on what a public servant is validly authorized to do. This criterion highlights and follows from another important feature of the very idea of government. Call this the *rule of law* component of responsibility. The legal code of a representative democracy specifies what a person – whether a citizen, a noncitizen community member, a public servant, or otherwise – may or may not do, full stop. If a policy worker is not, by some reasonable interpretation of the codes set forth, legally authorized to act in her official capacity in a way that would reinforce the values of representative democracy, it

---

[13] Zacka (2017, 37–42) argues that this kind of mechanistic description (the "rational systems perspective") of the job of a policy worker, which he calls the compliance model of public administration, forecloses the possibility of policy workers making politically legitimate normative judgment calls in their day-to-day work. We consider this an instance of the problem of inductive reasoning detailed in Sections 2.3 and 2.4 above. As we will demonstrate in more detail in Section 6, adherence to the complementarity principle bakes guidance on matters of normative discretion into administrative systems, which leaves open the possibility of both authorized and unauthorized normative discretion, a middle ground between unfettered normative discretion and no legitimate normative discretion at all. Hence, the term "authorized normative discretion" we use in the next paragraph is neither redundant nor an oxymoron.

is incumbent on her to refrain from taking that action, if only because to do so at one's discretion is to violate the terms of one's public office. It is to take matters into one's own hands, which is to step outside of the purview of one's official role.

Even if taking matters into one's own hands would *in fact* yield better consequences or better uphold the values of the system than would taking any course of action authorized to one's position, to do so would constitute a dereliction of duty. The ends do not justify the means. If they did, any policy worker would be authorized to act on the basis of his or her own judgments to secure whatever he or she alone determined to be the result that best squares with the values of the system, which even if he or she turned out to be right would be to unacceptably circumvent the public process by which public policy is chosen and by which constraints on public actions are determined, and to thereby undercut the duly determined will of the people. The ends must be achieved by *authorized* means – and only by authorized means – if social stability is to hold.

The rule of law component imposes the second limit on policy workers' authorized normative discretion; the values of the system impose the first. Together the individual duty and the rule of law components set the bounds within which one may perform one's role as a public servant responsibly. While the first two components of responsible policy work circumscribe what one *may* do in one's official capacity, the third deals entirely with what one *must* do.

The third and final criterion of responsible policy work says that "policy workers *must* act to reinforce values if they have the capability to use means that are, in fact, likely to succeed in reinforcement" (Bertelli 2021, 197). It is not a limit, but, rather, something of a propulsion mechanism. That is, policy workers are positively obligated to reinforce political values whenever it is possible, likely to succeed, and they are validly authorized to do so. Call this the *capability* component of responsibility. This criterion holds because the failure to reinforce political values when doing so is both possible and within one's purview as a public servant is an abdication of duty, which is no more permissible than executing functions beyond those legally authorized and delegated to one's office. Abdication of this kind threatens the sovereignty of the system from within. It would be as if a sentient bomb, having recently become a pacifist, declined to detonate and instead bonked its target with an ineffectual thud (Hofstadter 1981). Even if the outcome would have caused a great deal of destruction, if doing so would have reinforced the values of the political system that sent it, it ought to have detonated in accordance with its job description. To willfully abdicate (perhaps on the grounds of one's own deeply held values) is to defy one's duty to execute the functions duly and legally delegated to one's office. If you cannot or will not execute the functions delegated to you, you ought not hold the office at all. Resolving the problem of roles in this event means quitting the office.

When a policy worker does not have the means or authority to reinforce values, the criteria of responsibility respect the Kantian principle that "ought implies can," though they do so with some nuance that is worth exploring. Many strands of the normative literature in public administration incorporate more-or-less deontological intuitions about what policy workers ought to do for society, as our discussion of social equity in Section 4.3 exemplifies. Consider a claim that all of us, policy workers included, "ought to feed the hungry." There are certainly moments at which it would be impossible for a person to comply with this prescription, but the mandate to feed the hungry is *not* rendered void in these moments. Its normative force comes from the moral judgment that no one should have to suffer the psychological and physical consequences of hunger or to die for lack of basic necessities and so forth. Therefore, we should not feed the hungry only when we can, but always, and sometimes we will not be able to live up to what is morally required of us.

This speaks directly to claims that policy workers should "stand on principle." Consider an argument that a policy worker should hand over classified documents to foreign entities because the people ought to know the information within them, and they should get it by any means necessary. Suppose that handing over the documents goes beyond the physical capabilities of that policy worker, or that it would require that individual to act illegally, or that delivering the documents to a foreign agent would undermine a core value of the system in which the policy worker operates. The three components of responsibility incorporate an understanding of all these scenarios, showing that a policy worker can responsibly fail to live up to some deeper sense of duty. It provides a rationale for a policy worker defying broader ethical principles even when, all else equal, they could be upheld. While duty does imply power in responsible policy work, the power is not merely physical and is not absolute. It is both conferred and circumscribed by these considerations: You are obligated to act *if* you in fact can act (capability), *if* it would reinforce the values of the system (individual duty), *and if* it would not require you to exceed your legally circumscribed authority (rule of law). It is crucial to recognize that the individual duty and rule of law components of responsibility contribute directly to what it means for a policy worker to have the power to act.

Not one word of our discussion of responsibility should be read to mean that responsible policy work means upholding or complementing the values of any particular office holder, but rather the values of the system of which one's official function is a part. As our imagined President Eisenhower said, representative democracy does not necessitate that he, the President, should rule as a king, and that all policy workers are duty-bound to execute his vision. Instead, the system itself is imbued with certain values from the start, and those are the values with which policy workers' actions – and the actions of the President – are duty-bound to comport.

The infamous "Saturday Night Massacre" on October 20, 1973, which occurred during the Watergate scandal, illustrates what we have been arguing in the preceding paragraphs. Special Prosecutor Archibald Cox refused to abide by an agreement between the White House and the Senate Watergate Committee in regard to taped conversations after being ordered by President Nixon to do so. Cox explained himself in detail in a televised press conference wherein he was asked "is not your intention in direct conflict with the President's orders to you, and if it is and you're fired by the end of this news conference, what happens then?" He replied, "I was appointed by the Attorney General. Under the statutes, the Attorney General and those to whom he delegates authority are in charge of all litigation, including the obtaining of evidence. I think there is a question whether anyone other than the Attorney General can give me any instructions that I have any legal obligation to obey" (*New York Times* 1973a, 60). As a consequence, President Nixon ordered Attorney General Eliot Richardson to fire Cox.

Richardson, who had appointed Cox, refused to carry out that order and resigned, writing in his letter to Nixon:

> I specified that he would have "full authority" for "determining whether or not to contest the assertion of 'executive privilege' or any other testimonial privilege." And while the special prosecutor can be removed from office for "extraordinary improprieties," I also pledged that "the Attorney General will not countermand or interfere with the special prosecutor's decisions actions." While I fully respect the reasons that have led you to conclude that the special prosecutor must be discharged, I trust that you understand that I could not in the light of these firm and repeated commitments carry out your direction that this be done. (*New York Times* 1973b, 61)

Nixon then turned to Deputy Attorney General William Ruckelshaus with the same order and the same result. Ruckelshaus, in his resignation letter, said only that "my conscience will not permit me to carry out your instruction to discharge Archibald Cox" (*New York Times* 1973b, 61). Years later, he explained "I was convinced that Cox had only been doing what he had the authority to do; what was really of concern to the president and the White House was that he was too close. He hadn't engaged in any extraordinary improprieties, quite the contrary" (McFadden 2019).

Ruckelshaus's resignation made Solicitor General Robert Bork the Acting Attorney General, and Nixon wrote to him straightaway, ordering him to fire Cox who had "made it apparent that he will not comply with the instructions I issued to him . . . Clearly the government of the United States cannot function if employees of the executive branch are free to ignore in this fashion the instructions of the President" (Kilpatrick 1973, A1). Bork complied, Cox was fired and the FBI sealed his office as well as those of Richardson and Ruckelshaus.

While that night he said very little, years later, Bork explained his decision in an interview:

> The reason for the discharge was that I had, I thought, to contain a very dangerous situation, one that threatened the viability of the Department of Justice and of other parts of the executive branch. The President and Mr. Cox had gotten themselves, without my aid, into a position of confrontation. There was never any question that Mr. Cox, one way or another, was going to be discharged. At that point you would have had massive resignations from the top levels of the Department of Justice. If that had happened, the Department of Justice would have lost its top leadership, all of it, and would I think have effectively been crippled. (Noble 1987, A22)

The US District Court for the District of Columbia disagreed, holding that

> "Mr. Cox was not nominated by the President and did not serve at the President's pleasure. As an appointee of the Attorney General, Mr. Cox served subject to congressional rather than Presidential control . . . The firing of Archibald Cox in the absence of a finding of extraordinary impropriety was in clear violation of an existing Justice Department regulation having the force of law and was therefore illegal" *Nader v. Bork*, 366 F. Supp. 104, 107–108 (D.D.C. 1973).

In their statements above, Richardson, Ruckelshaus, and Bork base their claims to responsibility on an individual duty to reinforce the values of the United States government – namely, maintaining the lawful place of the Department of Justice and the President within it – by ensuring the stability of their system of government in a constitutional crisis. It is the rule of law component of responsibility that focuses our attention on the bounds of their authority. However, they apparently differed in their views about capability: Richardson and Ruckelshaus saw no "extraordinary impropriety" and thus could not act. Bork thought he was authorized to remove Cox, and he could successfully maintain constitutional values[14] by making the dismissal explicitly

---

[14] Richardson supported Bork's decision in later comments: "I had asked the legal counsel to check whether Nixon had the right to fire Cox. The legal counsel concluded that he did. Therefore, we thought Bork could do the right thing and deliver that message" (Noble 1987, A22).

on the President's direction and without reference to the "extraordinary impropriety" standard.[15] While a court later held that he did not have that authority, Bork seems to have acted on a belief that he did, and that belief completes his claim to responsible action. Believing that he acted responsibly would not have been enough to end the matter, of course. Had Archibald Cox sought reinstatement as Special Prosecutor after the decision in *Nader* v. *Bork* (which he did not), Bork could *not* have ignored the court's order and blocked him on the instructions of the President or his own view of responsible action. The rule of law and capability components would have come together in this instance to make such an act irresponsible as well as illegal.

Together, the individual duty, rule of law, and capability criteria offer a full description of responsible policy work. The first two describe the limitations on policy workers' discretion which follow from the political values of the system of government in which they operate; the third imposes a positive obligation to act when doing so reinforces those values. So long as a policy worker complies with these criteria, she is executing her official function responsibly. To assent to this description is to accept the first premise of the argument for complementarity. The truth (or at least the plausibility) of that premise established, we are free to move on to our second premise.

4 The Consequences of Irresponsible Policy Work

HECTOR: *Members of the CAB are committed to an equitable society and make good on that commitment in the limited sphere of aviation policy. Mr. President, they don't forget about democracy in America.*

EISENHOWER: *I'm afraid, Hector, if their own vision of an equitable society is guiding them, they might well be doing just that.*

HECTOR: *But, you can't be serious, Mr. President. Equality is a bedrock value in our democracy.*

EISENHOWER: *I'm deadly serious, Hector. You and your colleagues on the CAB don't get to decide what an equitable society looks like. That's for the people to decide and to express through the ballot box and through the actions of representatives they choose and reject. The Congress has the power to*

---

[15] Bork wrote on October 20, 1973: "Dear Mr. Cox: As provided by Title 28, Section 508(B) of the United States Code and Title 28, Section 132(A) of the Code of Federal Regulations, I have today assumed the duties of Acting Attorney General. In that capacity I am, as instructed by the President, discharging you, effective at once, from your position as special prosecutor, Watergate special prosecution force. Very truly yours, ROBERT H. BORK Acting Attorney General" (*New York Times* 1973b, 61).

create an agency that embodies that expression of an equitable society.

HECTOR: *Sir, the vote is such a blunt instrument. Government has to fill in the gaps, and that means taking a view on promoting values like equity that facilitate democracy rather than impede it.*

EISENHOWER: *We seem to have a very different understanding of democracy. I think it means rule by the people, and that means all of the people. And what about your claim before that my office should guide national policy? Are you suggesting that people like me and you should be determining both public policy and the character of our democracy?*

HECTOR: *Public servants have to do the work of making public policy happen, of filling in the details of vague directives in legislation to get things done. Trying to address every stakeholder is exactly what makes the CAB so inefficient in my view.*

EISENHOWER: *What you call inefficiencies are precisely the things that protect self-government. The Congress makes the laws, and that means they design the agencies, Hector – efficiency be damned if they want it to be damned. If it's hard to make policy on the CAB, the agency is probably doing a good job of coming to terms with a wide variety of views. You and I can have our views about air travel and how our government should work just like everybody else when we're enjoying our beef stew at the dinner table. But on the job, our views are no better than anyone else's. In domestic affairs, the Congress gives me some authority for making policy just like it gives some to you.*

HECTOR: *We can't consult everyone in the country as we make policy. How can we understand the views of those who are silent?*

EISENHOWER: *By talking to their representatives, both politicians and the organized interests, and by thinking about what's left out of the picture you get from them. Then you do your best and we representatives face accountability from the public. It's a pain in the neck, Hector, and the rules we have in this country are plenty complicated – and they don't always work that well – but that's what an agency has to do to serve the democracy.*

HECTOR: *What a mess!*

EISENHOWER: *I wouldn't have it any other way.*

The task of the next four sections (4.1–4.4) is to offer support for the second premise of the argument for the complementarity principle by demonstrating what happens when governance structures are not designed with the proper political values and their reinforcement in mind. To reiterate the premise in question, our claim as stated above is that "since responsible policy work requires workers to reinforce the political values of the system in which they operate, governance structures ought to be designed with the relevant political values and their reinforcement in mind."

We first consider a contemporary puzzle of public administration – that of identity and representation in policy work. We then consider and scrutinize a widely discussed solution to this puzzle called representative bureaucracy, which suggests that attending to concerns of social equity is and ought to be a primary aim of rank-and-file policy workers. Next, we contrast a focus on social equity in everyday policy work with the concept of fidelitous representation articulated in Section 3.2, which raises a question (and ventures an answer) as to the level at which it is appropriate to address problems of social equity. We then turn to other forms of representative agency to illustrate the problem we see with the current locus of action for equitable outcomes.

4.1 Identity and Representation in Policy Work

Theories of *representative bureaucracy* posit a link between a particular group identification on the part of policy workers and a bias in the use of those workers' discretion that favors the groups with which they identify. Consider a social identity group A, for example, women, Latin@ people, immigrants, veterans. Three claims prevail in the literature.

First, a claim of *passive representation* is that the proportion of policy workers identifying with A should reflect the proportion of A-identifiers in the polity. Writing in the United Kingdom, Kingsley (1944) considered the issue to be class, and passive representation beyond the Oxbridge elite in the civil service was the object of his argument. In the United States, Long (1952, 811) begins from a premise that the value of pluralism, of a political order in which everyone in the polity can participate, is crucial for the state to embrace, but "[i]mportant and vital interests in the United States are unrepresented, underrepresented, or malrepresented in Congress." His view is that "[t]hese interests receive more effective and more responsible representation through administrative channels than through the legislature" (811). What legitimates representation at the administrative level of the state, for Long, is the value of responsiveness. Saltzstein (1979, 469) clarifies, "the position taken by such proponents is that bureaucracy will be responsive to the interests and desires of important social groups in society if its personnel are drawn proportionately from these social groups and share the same values and attitudes as the groups they represent." This happens, writes Meier (1975, 528), because the mirroring of social identity groups among the cast of policy workers means that "the decisions made by the bureaucracy will be similar to the decisions made if the entire American public passed on the issue." Social equity, on this view, demands that the community of policy workers becomes a microcosm of the pluralistic interests – proxied by the social identity groups – in the polity with the discretion to do policy work that is responsive to all those interests.

Second, a claim of *active representation* contends that A-identifiers hold "particular sets of values that, when better represented in the bureaucracy, translate into better policy and administrative outcomes" for A-identifiers in the polity (Riccucci and Van Ryzin 2016, 23). As voiced in the representative bureaucracy literature, this claim is a positive, rather than a normative one. Relevant bureaucratic discretion and within-group similarities in policy objectives provide the opportunity for transforming passive to active representation in policy work (24). When active representation occurs, scholars in this tradition contend that the public administration "becomes a representative organization that may *supplement* the representation provided through other political institutions including elected legislatures" (Bradbury and Kellough 2011, 158, emphasis added). Active representation is not a full-on revolution from within the bureaucracy from this perspective, but both a complement and supplement to the lawmaking of the elected representatives of the people with the goal of embedding pluralism into administration, that is, "Democracy denotes *all* of the people, not just some . . . those who may not otherwise receive effective service provisions through traditional political mechanisms can rely on career bureaucrats to the extent that passive and active representation are linked" (Riccucci and Van Ryzin 2016, 24).

A third claim is that of *symbolic representation*, which holds that "the mere existence of a passively represented bureaucracy . . . can produce a sense of trust and legitimacy among citizens who share those social origins resulting in cooperation from the citizens and ultimately the production of more effective policy outcomes" (Riccucci and Van Ryzin 2016, 25). By manifesting trust in administrative processes, the claim is that the symbolism of passive representation legitimates policy workers' efforts to act consistent with the wants of A-identifiers, bringing pluralism into the government as A-identifiers interact with other groups in government, shaping all policy workers' perspectives and their policy work in the process.

These theoretical claims suppose that isomorphic group identification between members of the public and the pool of policy workers in public administration should translate to better representation of relevant group-related interests in public policy one way or another, for one reason or another. Though there is some empirical evidence to support this supposition, that evidence is (perhaps inevitably) piecemeal and inconsistent. At this point, the problem with relying on inductive normative reasoning becomes acute. The evidence that, in certain circumstances, the inclusion of in-group identifiers among decision-makers can secure desirable results for in-group members does not imply that, for every group identity issue, the inclusion of in-group members in the decision-making body will do the same. While noting and cataloging successful implementations of the in-group policy-making strategy is good as a matter of positive social science, the normative conclusion, explicit or implicit, that more isomorphic group identification *improves* the representation of all the people in the process of policymaking is not warranted on the basis of the available evidence. The problem lies in the initial supposition which oversimplifies the necessarily diverse and complex constellation of factors that go into determinations of interests and the reasons for pursuing or promoting some interests over others.

The group-identity-to-group-representation supposition essentially sets up at least one of the following unsupported inferences:

1. Identity group membership implies representation;
2. Identity group membership implies trust;
3. Trust implies representation.

Both passive and active representation claims make the first kind of inference. Passive representation does this axiomatically: A-identifiers represent A-identifiers. Active representation does so with an inductive generalization: A-identifying policy workers have done their work so as to provide greater (or more frequent) benefits to A-identifiers when compared with non-A-identifying policy workers, which implies that A-identifiers represent A-identifiers. But mere membership in the same identity group does not guarantee identical interests, similar sets of interests, or even overlapping interests. Shelby (2007) argues, for instance, that there is little reason to suspect that there exists a sufficient overlap in the substantive values and interests of Black people (whether in a single country or worldwide) to establish a robust conception of a Black political identity (1–23). Still, the fact that there is no monolithic Black experience – that "individual or group differentiation within the black population" exists and "that there are many, perhaps incommensurable, ways to be black" (3) – does not preclude a kind of Black solidarity. It just means that Black representation in public offices does not guarantee that the interests of individual Black people will be better represented, either actively or passively. There are simply too many differences among intra-group interests to expect that kind of outcome. The same kind of problem exists for both the establishment of trust (inference 2) and the achievement of better representation through symbolic representation (inference 3). It is not enough to establish trust between A-identifiers and institutions of government that some number of people holding public offices or working in public administration are themselves A-identifiers.

A related problem is associated with the logical importance of trust for inferences 2 and 3. Even if shared identity is sufficient to establish for some a kind of (perhaps misguided) trust by in-group members, observing that one does in fact trust those who share one's identity does *not* imply that one's interests will be better represented in the public sphere by those who share their group identity. One can be a woman *and* a misogynist, and acting on the latter trait, one can institute policies that might work against the interests of some large contingent of people who identify as women. Clearly, being of the same social identity group is not only insufficient to establish trust, it does not, by itself, warrant trust. In the absence of a much stronger connection between identity and shared interests, and without being able to ground trust or representation in identity, these kinds of representation ought not to be expected to generate the outcomes proponents claim – at least not at the scale at which they envision.

One other important unifying thread running through these theories of representative bureaucracy – one we address more substantially in the pages to come – is the somewhat cynical presumption of failure at the level of representative government. The assumption is that representative government is incapable of responding to particularized, group-differentiated interests. Basically, it assumes institutional failures of sensitivity to certain public interests as a standard hazard of broader democratic procedures. Rather than offering a way to shore up these real or perceived shortcomings (or democratic deficits) at the governmental level, these theories offer a sort of resigned remedy ex post – a shortcut that evades, or an end run around, presupposed inevitable failures. In a sense, this avenue of remedy is democracy-defeating, because it accepts certain failures of representation (or representational cracks) as intractable consequences of large-scale democratic processes. Proponents of these views have more or less conceded that democracy is inadequate to its greater purpose and in need of ad hoc repairs, stitches, or bandages to hold together its broken pieces. This observation brings us to a deeper discussion of what we call the problem of levels.

4.2 The Problem of Levels

The pursuit of social equity in public administration is a frequent justification for violating the criteria for responsible policy work that we described in the preceding section. A prominent school of thought holds that it is part of a policy worker's job to use her discretion to strive for social equity in the everyday administration of public goods and services. Ultimately, we take the imperative to achieve social equity through day-to-day policy work to be obviated by the novel concept that we have introduced, and continue to defend, in the pages of this essay: fidelitous representation. We understand fidelitous representation to be a bedrock value and an essential component of any well-functioning representative democracy. It is, in a sense, an obvious precondition of such systems, but its obviousness has somehow gone unnoticed. As we said at the outset, there is real value in bringing what ought to be relatively obvious into sharper relief.

Fidelitous representation seems an obvious precondition of a well-functioning system of representative government because without it, the system is only nominally, as opposed to actually, representative. In its absence, the system cannot be legitimately representative. Surely, the very idea of representative government implies fidelitous representation. Nevertheless, the essential role of fidelitous representation in the concept of representative government is all too often overlooked. This essay demonstrates the benefits of bringing this value into the light. For one thing, it explains why building (unguided) normative discretion on issues of social equity into rank-and-file policy work risks directing public servants to behave irresponsibly. Doing so shifts the locus of legitimate social justice concerns from what we take to be the proper level of representatives, institutions, and institutional designers to the ground floor, so to speak, where such concerns can and, on the competing view, should be addressed by policy workers, according to their own views. Notice how this directly engages the problem of roles that we have spelled out above.

The disconnect lies in the pursuit of social equity at one's professional, but unguided, discretion and the pursuit of social equity at one's discretion as specified by institutional design. If value-congruity is built into the institution by design and the system itself values equity and diversity (as representative democracy does as a consequence of its commitments to equal voice and reasonable pluralism), then there will be fewer opportunities for policy workers to violate the conditions of responsible policy work in pursuit of social equity because those kinds of concerns are already built into what it means for the institution to function properly. We call this the *problem of levels*:

> Policy workers in democratic institutions are charged with enacting policies that can affect people's lives for better or worse. Consequently, they must

routinely make value judgments about how best to achieve the aims of their offices in ways that are to the public good. Absent guidance as to how to prioritize or adjudicate between competing values, policy workers must make these routine judgments at their own, unguided discretion, and in so doing, risk engaging in irresponsible policy work.

The problem of roles articulated in Section 3.3 draws out the problem of levels. As we have argued, it is not part of the role of a policy worker, when acting in her official capacity as a policy worker, to use her own judgment subject only to her own, unguided discretion to pursue whatever she sees as legitimate aims in her day-to-day work. Doing so means running the risk of engaging in either ultra vires activities (violating the rule of law component) or efforts that are out of step with the actual values of the system (violating the individual duty component of responsible policy work). But the contemporary focus in public administration on issues of social equity advises policy workers to do just that: to use their own judgment and their own (unguided) professional discretion to pursue what they see as legitimate social equity aims in their day-to-day work. Rank-and-file policy workers need guidance, grounded in a stable and uniform set of values, as to what social equity means and what measures to achieve it should look like if they are going to pursue such ends as a matter of routine policy work. That guidance can only come from the higher-order values embedded in the system of government within which one's department or agency is situated. This goal is achievable by clearly connecting democratic values to what is meant by social equity.

4.3 Social Equity in Public Administration

The argument for active bureaucratic representation relies on a concept of social equity that is unclearly defined. Attempts by public administration scholars to define social equity have produced a variety of conceptually vague, often inconsistent, and sometimes contradictory descriptions of the term. Writes Frederickson (1971, 311), "the procedures of representative democracy presently operate in a way that either fails or only very gradually attempts to reverse systematic discrimination against disadvantaged minorities. Social equity, then, includes activities designed to enhance the political power and economic well-being of these minorities." In 2000, a panel of the National Academy of Public Administration tautologically called it "The fair, just and *equitable* management of all institutions serving the public directly or by contract, and the fair, just and *equitable* distribution of public services, and implementation of public policy, and the commitment to promote fairness, justice, and *equity* in the formation of public policy" (Svara and Brunet 2004, 101, emphasis added).

This confusing state of affairs was apparent to Rosenbloom (2005, 248), who found it "worrisome for a term that gained prominence in the field of public administration as far back as 1968." He was concerned, as we are, with the use of the elusive idea to influence policy work, writing that in the United States, "[c]learly, public administrators need a mandate from the constitutional branches of government to legitimate their pursuit of redistribution and social change, just as they would to justify repression in the name of administrative efficiency or national security" (251).

The conceptual confusion arises from several sources (for details on each of the following descriptions, see Levinson et al. 2022, 2–11). First, social equity is sometimes described in terms of conflicting notions of *equality*: in terms of equal access, equal opportunity, or equal outcomes. Sometimes, it is couched in terms of equal respect, experience, or treatment. Sometimes, it is described in terms of *just distribution*, demanding in some cases a "fair" distribution of resources, or in others the equal distribution of outcomes across populations. And still other times, it is described in terms of the *priority of the less advantaged*, sometimes according to relative disadvantage, sometimes according to absolute disadvantage. More often than not, a single source's definition of the term will contain two or more of these characterizations, and more often than one might expect, two or more of them that stand in tension with one another, are incompatible, or are mutually inconsistent (Levinson et al. 2022, 10–11; see also Rosenbloom 2005).

The common thread present throughout these various descriptions of the concept consists of (a) the recognition of some kind of connection (either merely correlational or causal, or both) between certain morally irrelevant social differences (race, socioeconomic status, disability, etc.) and disparate social outcomes, along with (b) a goal of severing that connection in order to eliminate the disparate outcomes. What is unclear even to social equity advocates and scholars, it appears, is whether the connection to be severed is one of mere correlation or one of causation and whether severing the connection can actually be expected to successfully eliminate the disparities in social outcomes.

Scholars and advocates often come to endorse conflicting aims under the same umbrella term because they are trying to accommodate multiple possibilities. This is especially well illustrated by mission statements that advocate for both equal treatment and equal outcomes.[16] Consider the goals of equal

---

[16] Principle 4 of the American Society of Public Administration Code of Ethics (www.aspanet.org/ASPA/Code-of-Ethics/ASPA/Code-of-Ethics/Code-of-Ethics) states that its members have a commitment to "Treat all persons with fairness, justice, and equality and respect individual differences, rights, and freedoms. Promote affirmative action and other initiatives to reduce unfairness, injustice, and inequality in society."

treatment, as expressed through equality of opportunity, and equal outcomes. If being treated to the same opportunities for success fails to produce equally successful outcomes, presumably, we ought to engineer the right outcomes, but to do so, we will be forced to engage in disparate treatment. Why not just aim to engineer the right outcomes from the start? If the connection is causal, treating people to equal opportunities for success should help to eliminate the disparities in outcomes. If the connection is merely correlational, engineering equal outcomes may be the only way to eliminate the social disparities at issue. A presumption in favor of earned positive outcomes might explain the double-dipping. Still, when people advocate for "social equity" without specifying more clearly what they mean by it, what they mean to achieve, or the means by which they mean to achieve it, "[they] risk misleading [themselves] and others about the values for which [they] stand ... [and] also risk sidestepping the hard judgments and potential trade-offs" (Levinson et al. 2022, 22–23) that are inextricable to the design of good governance structures – that which enables and encourages policy workers to act responsibly. Hence, what appears to be lacking in the public ethos is an authoritative specification (or series of specifications) as to what we as a polity mean by "social equity," what we mean to achieve in the pursuit of it, and the means by which it is legitimate to pursue it. Without these details, policy workers lack the guidance necessary to obviate reliance on their personal value sets in determining how best to pursue equitable outcomes. That is, they are left – or worse, *led* – to engage in potentially irresponsible policy work.

According to Raz (2006), one feature of legitimate authority is that it preempts other reasons for action. That is, the fact that some action would comply with an authoritative directive takes the place of other reasons for or against taking that action; the fact that it would comply with an authoritative directive is not merely added to the balance of other reasons for or against doing it (Raz 2006, 1018–1019). Determinations of the legitimacy of any purported source of authority are and must be made by individuals, but these determinations are not made in a vacuum. Relevant structural norms help a person to decide whether an authority is legitimate or not. In the case of public administration, a person taking on the role of a policy worker must accept as authoritative the laws and the values of the system. When assuming the role of a policy worker and accepting these sources of authority, one also implicitly accepts the preemptive nature of any and all authoritative directives that issue from these sources. It is those sources – the system's values and laws – that must determine the character, the relative importance, and the legitimate avenues of pursuit of matters of social equity in public administration if uniformity and consistency in such pursuits are to prevail.

One might understandably worry at this point that the very problem policy workers are confronting and trying to solve in using their (unguided) discretion to advance social equity is the inaction, or worse, the counteraction, on such issues at the higher levels of government. Laws are made by elected representatives, many of whom have no (politically motivated or constituency-induced) interest in advancing the goals of social equity, and institutional designers have other concerns when deciding how any given agency or institution will function. The very reasons public administration scholarship tends to foreground the pursuit of social equity at the unguided discretion of policy workers are (a) the failure at higher levels to attend to such issues and (b) the positions of policy workers, who must facilitate such pursuits, relative to the public.

The first reason is a failure in practice; it does not indicate a deeper shortcoming in our argument so far. If anything, it illustrates the heretofore (incredibly) nonobvious nature of the value of fidelitous representation. Should that value be acted on and reinforced as it should at every level of a representative democratic system, the impetus behind leaving important and difficult determinations on issues of social equity to the (again, professional but unguided) discretion of street-level workers would disappear. The second reason counts in favor of our proposed resolution to this practical failure. That fidelitous representation is hard and sometimes not achieved cannot justify the substitution of unguided policy work. Perhaps this statement has seemed obvious enough to political philosophers to make them less interested in discretionary policy work than they have been until recently.[17] Treating the arguments of public administration scholars carefully, which we are doing presently, makes it clear that fidelitous representation demands more attention than it has received by either scholarly community.

Policy workers are in fact those who must execute social equity pursuits in public administration; they are not, however, those who must or ought to be deciding on the substantive details of what those pursuits should be or aim to achieve. Our proposed resolution has already been set out in these pages: It is adherence to complementarity by embedding in governance structures expectations regarding the representative democratic value of fidelitous representation. Failure to attend to issues of social equity is a failure to represent with fidelity. Building expectations of fidelitous representation into what it means to do one's job as a representative correctly – in line with the specified functions of the office – orients substantive social equity concerns to the level of governance

---

[17] Engster (2020, 622) observes that "most liberal and republican theorists" contend that "bureaucratic discretion should be sharply constrained, oriented around fixed rules, and exercised impersonally for the sake of maintaining limited and responsive government in the implementation of laws and policies" (see also Heath 2020).

at which they ought to operate. Once the relevant determinations are made at the appropriate level, rank-and-file policy workers have the guidance necessary to use their (guided) discretion to responsibly pursue issues of social equity. This does not make for a representative bureaucracy in the usual sense, but for a *responsible* one.

Recall that fidelitous representation involves actively preserving the salience of and responding with positive action to competing public interests within one's constituency. This is a core democratic value implied by the characterization of democracy as government of the people, by the people, and for the people, where "the people" encompasses the whole population of the polity. Recall as well that we are trying to show that adherence to complementarity is indispensable to good governance structure design, where such "good" design means designing public agencies and their procedures to facilitate responsible policy work, and thus "administer democracy" (Bertelli 2021). In this sense, our project here uses certain ideals (e.g., fidelitous representation) as ultimate aims which in turn prescribe appropriate actions in real-world (and thus, nonideal) circumstances. Our point is that the solution to the failure at the higher levels of government to attend to issues of social equity is not to accept that failure and resort to delegating responsibility for such concerns down the chain to policy workers (see, e.g., Zacka 2017, 62–65). If the designers of governance structures adhered to the complementarity principle, and thus agencies were imbued with an expectation of fidelitous representation from the start, pursuits of social equity by policy workers would be less likely to result in ultra vires actions or in actions that defy or fail to uphold the individual duty and capability components of responsible policy work. This is because they would have stable guidance as to what it means to pursue issues of social equity in line with their roles as policy workers.

Notice that policy work that reinforces the democratic value of fidelitous representation resolves the problem of levels by strengthening the notion that questions of social equity need to be set at the level of representatives, institutions, and institutional designers. In so doing, it also helps to ease the tensions and internal struggles inherent to the problem of roles. If policy workers have express guidance on these issues, which themselves issue from the values of representative government, their own personal values need not enter their deliberations about what to do in any given situation. Because the values of the system, including the values of social equity and its legitimate avenues of pursuit, have been built into the governance structure within which policy work occurs, a policy worker is better positioned to act responsibly – that is, to choose a course of action that reinforces the values of the system and that falls within her legally authorized purview – to achieve what have been deemed (through the appropriate democratic channels) to be publicly desirable, socially equitable ends. If a circumstance arises that presents an as-yet unsettled question, she is better positioned to responsibly refrain from immediate action, and to decisively kick the question back up the chain of decision-making. An expectation of fidelitous representation built into the governance structure gives her solid footing from which to make demands of her superiors. A well-designed institution is one that facilitates responsible policy work – one in which governance values complement or reinforce the values of the larger political system. Thus, a well-designed institution is one that builds in expectations about and mechanisms which reinforce the value of fidelitous representation. Recall that Cassidy Hutchinson had a well-designed institution, namely, the January 6th Committee, but Edward Snowden did not. Notice that this also preserves the accountability of representatives to the public. Accountability for any street-level policy worker's responsible course of action does not (as well it should not) fall on the policy worker. It is her job to carry out the orders given by her superiors (i.e., by elected representatives), and thus it is her superiors who are accountable for the outcomes.

Advocates of social equity as a guiding principle of public administration might argue that even in a pluralistic democracy characterized by fidelitous representation, the practice of fidelitous representation must be calculated on majoritarian grounds which will crowd out the genuine availability of certain valuable life options for minority groups. The only way to counter this is to design governance structures that actively attend to membership in the relevant groups in ways that defy the majoritarian principle at the heart of democracy.

What this line of argument gets wrong is the assumption that the value of majoritarianism enjoys an insuperable centrality in the concept of democracy. The value of pluralism is not superficial – it has teeth, and these two legitimately democratic values can – and often do – run up against each other because an essential feature of democratic pluralism is its grounding in autonomy. Trade-offs between these values must be made if autonomy is to be respected.

Schouten (2019) has recently argued not just for the permissibility, but, rather, for a positive obligation on the behalf of modern democratic governments to promote certain substantive and indeed group-differentiated interests on liberal democratic, substantive-value-neutral grounds. Her argument essentially constitutes a rebuttal to the view that democracy is incapable of responding to concerns about social equity. We have reasons that are neutral with respect to substantive values, she argues, to promote autonomy because autonomy is necessary for and essential to democratic governance (Schouten 2019, 170–197). Basically, in the absence of an autonomous populace, one in which people freely and independently decide on and pursue their own conceptions of the good life, democratic inputs are of little value. They simply do not and cannot express the interests of the people because the interests of the people are not being decided upon by the people. Consequently, the preservation and indeed the *promotion of autonomy* is itself a substantively neutral, purely political, democratic value. Democracy as we understand it is simply impossible without it.

Genuine autonomy, though, requires having a sufficient number of good options from which to choose (Raz 1986). A person without stable housing, for instance, cannot make a genuinely autonomous decision between sleeping out in the cold or taking refuge in a crowded shelter where she will have a roof over her head, but is likely to be assaulted or robbed in the night. As the saying goes, she is stuck between a rock and a hard place. The adage itself acknowledges that this kind of decision is, in a very real sense, no decision at all. To be forced into choosing any single option from a pool of only bad options is to have one's autonomy effectively denied. Notice that not much about the situation changes when one is free to choose the only good option from a pool of otherwise bad options. That option essentially becomes the only option. To choose it is not exactly to make an autonomous decision. Just how many good options must exist for the whole pool of options to contain a "sufficient number" of them is unclear, but certain kinds of practical considerations can help to bring an answer into focus.

On Schouten's view, one such consideration is the fact that there are certain valuable and in fact widely valued ways of life that people cannot enact because they are not genuinely available options (Schouten 2019). She argues that if a way of life is valued widely enough or, perhaps, is simply a genuinely valuable one, and is also widely foreclosed as an option, a person's autonomy is thereby thwarted or denied. That alone is bad from a democratic perspective given that autonomy is essential to democracy, but when one considers the potential social consequences of a widespread denial of autonomy, the threat to social stability becomes clear (198–227). The upshot of Schouten's argument is that government interventions to promote the enactment of widely valued (and perhaps genuinely valuable) ways of life are warranted on purely democratic, autonomy promoting grounds, and that subsidization is one kind of intervention that might be warranted (Schouten 2019, 170–227).

Notice that, according to this argument, substantive interests based on social difference may be the proper locus of concern for policy workers. Schouten's (2019) argument is, after all, about the gendered division of labor. She defends the claim that government action to promote gender egalitarianism in the home is permissible on grounds that are neutral with respect to substantive values.

Certain ways of life are systematically prohibitively costly for members of different minority groups. And though not all valuable or widely valued ways of life must be available at equal cost, they do have to be within reach to be genuinely available options (Schouten 2019, 170–197). Seeing a way of life as a live option depends on seeing it enacted by people like you, but when it becomes apparent that a particularly valuable and widely valued way of life is out of reach for a large contingent of the population, it threatens social harmony which, in turn, constitutes a threat to social stability. Since all of these (social stability, the ability to choose and to pursue one's own conception of the good, governmental support for and reinforcement of value pluralism in society, and so forth) are primary democratic values, this kind of scenario ultimately licenses certain social-equity-based pursuits – things like affirmative action policies, which bring certain social forms into reach for members of groups for whom they would otherwise be out of reach on autonomy promoting grounds, and without the need for governance structures that objectionably undercut democratic values by directing policy workers to make decisions about what constitutes an equitable solution at their own, unguided discretion. The difference is in the level of governance at which it is appropriate to attend to social equity concerns like access, opportunity, and equitable social outcomes.

Schouten offers an independent line of reasoning that supports our conclusion that the appropriate level for deciding on legitimate aims and pursuits of social equity in a democracy is the level of institutional design, not the level of policy work, by grounding the warrant for governmental interventions on issues of equity in *political* values (e.g., democratic values) as opposed to in the *substantive* value sets of individual policy workers. The public supplies the input as to what kinds of options ought to be available, and institutional designers determine how to make that happen. Public-facing policy workers ought to carry out their discretionary duties within the bounds that have been set and according to the determinations that have been made in the proper, substantive-value-neutral way.

The lynchpin for the democratic legitimacy of pursuits of social equity is the democratic value of pluralism. Democracies value pluralism because they value and respect a genuine diversity of values, opinions, and inputs, all of which are necessary for genuine democratic rule. They could not genuinely value and respect these things if they did not also genuinely value and respect the diversity of persons, personal histories, and other background conditions (socio-economic, cultural, racial, and so forth) that give rise to those values, opinions, and inputs. People must be able to determine their own interests, and those interests need to be taken into consideration in order for a government to be genuinely democratic. Thus, it is in the government's interest to preserve, perhaps even to promote, a diverse, autonomous *demos*. Insofar as pursuits of social equity in public administration contribute to that aim, they are democratically licensed, but since they are a part of public policy, they must also be specified, circumscribed, and initiated by democratic mechanisms.

4.4 Representative Bureaucracy and the Problem of Levels

Recall that advocates of both passive and passive-to-active representation as tools for enhancing social equity tend to assume that people of a particular social identity group have higher stakes in the members of that identity group's outcomes than do nonmembers. It is therefore imperative to design agencies such that they are largely composed of in-group identifiers and often, according to some theorists, such that the selected representatives that make up the organization are tasked with policymaking that affects in-group identifiers (Fung 2003). This, they argue, frequently makes for better policy outcomes for in-group identifiers than would any other governance structure design. But even if it *does* make for better policy outcomes, it defies the democratic value of deference to the collective will, which constitutes an irresponsible execution of public policy work. As Lafont (2020) would observe, it "shortcuts" democracy. The representatives making policy in such agencies are not elected representatives, but appointed ones. They are neither bound by nor accountable to the will of the electorate (of which they, presumably, are just one part), and their independent choices are not necessarily bound to improve outcomes.

Aiming for fidelitous representation through targeted policies like affirmative action, by contrast, builds the relevant stakes into what it means for the agency to function properly, all the while maintaining both accountability and deference to the collective will. Regardless of the demographic makeup of the representative agency, the desired outcomes determined according to the collective will constitute the policy goal, and if the desired outcomes are meant to counteract systemic disadvantages associated with a particular social identity group, the result should be comparably advantageous for that group. Does this way of grounding group-differentiated policy goals proliferate the possibilities for legitimate government interventions that promote substantively valuable and contested ways of life? Yes, but so what? If such interventions are licensed by the democratic values of the state and the polity the agency serves – as we have argued they should be – it is possible to attend to the kinds of concerns championed by advocates of social equity without engaging in irresponsible policy work or violating the complementarity principle.

Value-congruity distinguishes the actions of a fidelitous representative enact-ing, or working together with other representatives to enact, a policy that addresses such concerns at the policy level, within the parameters permitted by law and democratic principles, from the actions of an administrator in the Department of Motor Vehicles deciding to adjudicate between equally qualified applicants for a job on the basis of membership in a given identity group. The law and the principles of a representative democracy collectively circumscribe which possible means to the desired ends count as legitimate and which do not. When those constraints are ignored in the interest of achieving "good" out-comes by any means necessary, the result is a kind of policy work that is potentially corrosive to the system it aims to serve, rather than one that is complementary to its values.

Social equity has been seen as one of the "pillars" of public administration (Frederickson 1980). We contend that it can only be so inasmuch as it is built into the governance structures in which policy work is done, and this means that it must confront the problem of levels. When managers have the authority to hire a diverse workforce, reasonable pluralism suggests they ought to do so. The manner and extent to which that diverse workforce should improve outcomes for previously underrepresented groups depends on the authority they have *qua* policy workers to make such improvements, not on their own decisions about the substance of those improvements. Active representation through policy work must resolve the problem of levels by gaining the endorsement of repre-sentatives. Bureaucrats seeking to achieve active representation must offer proposals to both representatives and the people for governance structures and administrative procedures that embody their understanding of social equity. If they are adopted, these ideas can be *legitimately* revolutionary as they can bring valuable ways of life into the grasp of more people, enhancing pluralism through the fidelitous representation of elected representatives, who can judge their connection to the wants of the people. However, it is crucial to recognize that in a democracy, the people make the choices about options for the good life, not the policy workers. Representatives must continue to represent with fidelity when designing how to make all options possible, and they must face account-ability for their choices about the means, not just the ends of policy work. An *illegitimate* revolution occurs when policy workers take autonomy away from the people, making and implementing the options themselves without the constraints imposed by a requirement of fidelitous representation and violating the rule of law requirement of responsible policy work. Should a representative bureaucracy encourage this, it would seek to do something undemocratic, while adhering to all the conditions of responsible action we have discussed will keep that from happening.

5 The Consequences of Nonfidelitous Representation

HECTOR: *Mr. President, don't you think you're being a good bit too formalistic about the demands of democracy? It seems as though you don't allow an agency like the CAB to ask the public anything directly. We need advice from those we serve to function effectively.*

EISENHOWER: *Seeking advice is absolutely fine. But taking advice isn't representing in the sense of our democracy. Advice can help you do your job, but we have the rule of law in this country and advice doesn't justify an end run around the Congress, Hector.*

HECTOR: *Sir, Section 306 of the Civil Aeronautics Act of 1938 allows the CAB to "study the possibilities of the development of air commerce and of the aeronautical industry,"[18] and when we do that, we get advice from people in that very industry as a matter of course. Suppose we were to check with a group of citizens who live near the airports that we would have to expand in any development plan. Wouldn't that make the agency behave more democratically?*

EISENHOWER: *Well, what do you mean when you say you'd check with them? If you mean get their advice about how much expansion would impact their communities, then it is perfectly appropriate. If you mean that they could veto the plans because they don't like them, no, Hector, it's not more democratic.*

HECTOR: *Then suppose that they're not just people who live near airports, but a random draw of everyone in the country. Surely that group represents the public and can stop us from going too far?*

EISENHOWER: *A random draw? Mox nix, Hector! That group is not the people, and the members of Congress represent all of the people. So do I, and when I engage in foreign affairs, where the Congress and the courts give me latitude, I have to think about all the people when I take action. The CAB doesn't have the authority to let a randomly drawn group of Americans make some of its decisions. That group can advise, but it can't decide.*

---

[18] 52 Stat. 986 (1938).

HECTOR:	But, Mr. President, it's a representative sample, and we would be kidding ourselves if we thought that the Congress does a perfect job of representing minority groups.
EISENHOWER:	Do you think that representing people on some characteristics you can easily account for, like their race or their age, is the same thing as representing what they want? Nothing requires that another man at the age of 70 wants the same thing from his government as I do. Nothing at all, Hector. The representation we who are elected have to do is not an exercise in statistics, but an honest effort to understand what the people would want our policies to be. If we get it wrong, they'll throw us out. And if we don't make that honest effort, we shouldn't be in office at all.
HECTOR:	I understand, Mr. President, but that certainly does weaken the authority the CAB has to do what Congress expects.
EISENHOWER:	Congress can expect the CAB to use the authority it has and nothing more. You and your colleagues can't give it to me or to a group of business executives, or your random group of citizens. Congress might be able to do some of that, but the Congress and FDR had a lesson in the particulars of our democracy when they tried that business route, didn't they?[19]
HECTOR:	I had thought of that as a rather formal constitutional question rather than a democratic one until now.
EISENHOWER:	The Constitution contains the stuff of our democracy, and we've been learning what it all means over the last 170 years. But when you're in this office, Hector, the people are your focus, and the Constitution enables and limits what you can do to help them govern themselves.
HECTOR:	The CAB has more constraints, but it, too, is part of that scheme of self-government.
EISENHOWER:	You called that scheme inefficient when we started this conversation.
HECTOR:	And you made it clear that it's the scheme we have, Mr. President.

At this juncture, one might express the concern that this all sounds fine in principle, but in practice, fidelitous representation is rare, and given its rarity, we are sometimes justified in taking steps that are not necessarily authorized by the public will to combat social ills through public policy work. What if

---

[19] *A.L.A. Schechter Poultry Corp.* v. *United States*, 295 U.S. 495 (1935).

representing the people with fidelity requires that a representative downplay a policy issue or even refrain from submitting it for public consent during a political campaign? Though elected in a district where no one cares about (or there is opposition to) enhancing workforce opportunities for immigrant laborers, the representative hopes to be able to help people in *another* district, where many immigrant laborers suffer, but where there is little chance of electing someone who will advocate for more work opportunities.[20] Can this representative, in a sense, *bypass* the will of the voters in her constituency by disproportionately weighting the interests of another representatives constituents over her own? The answer must take the form: Yes, so long as what one is doing reinforces the values of the system in which one operates. One way to ensure that it does so is to make use of a representative agency to help determine the right way to execute the public policy the representative has in mind.

To be clear, our use of the term "representative agency" here indicates a type of agency composed of members of the general public who will play some official role in the creation or adoption of a particular public policy (Bertelli 2021, 110–111). They are one form of what Klijn and Skelcher (2007, 587) call governance networks, which engage in "public policy-making and implementation through a web of relationships between government, business and civil society actors." Making use of this kind of agency might help an elected representative execute her policy agenda in numerous ways. Two potential models of representative agency, characterized below according to how each employs a representative-based deliberative processes, offer fertile ground for comparison. They show the difference between adhering to and failing to adhere to the principle of complementarity when designing governance structures. The difference lies in the nature and objectives of deliberation with and among the involved citizens.

5.1 *Cool v. Hot Deliberation in Representative Agency*

Ansell (2011, 168) describes a system of "collaborative governance" in terms of "fruitful conflict," that is, "conflict that in some manner enhances or advances knowledge, understanding, meaning, or capacity between different or opposing perspectives and interests." The examples that he marshals involve the creation of temporary "public agencies" (representative agencies), which draw participants from local publics, and which facilitate a deliberative process between parties with conflicting interests to arrive at a better understanding of the stakes at issue in the circumstances. The goal is not necessarily consensus, nor is it to hash out a winning and losing policy position. Rather, the goal is for the party

---

20 Our thanks to Meira Levinson for raising this line of questioning.

entrusted by the public with the power to devise and to execute public policy on a particular issue, be it a local representative or the manager of an independent agency, to acquire more fine-grained information in order to better address the issue.

Within his representative agencies, Ansell (2011) advocates for *cool deliberation*, in which deliberators have strong opposing opinions, responsive debate (designed to come to an agreement or an understanding rather than to win, all-or-nothing), and low stakes: The outcomes of these representative ("public") agencies are evaluable decisions to be used as input for policy-making decisions at the appropriate level. Klijn and Skelcher (2007, 588) see this as the sort of model that emphasizes pluralism, consisting, as it does, of "horizontal inter-dependencies through which actors steer the development of policy and its implementation." They contrast it with networks that are "centres of power and privilege that give structural advantage to particular private interests" because of their "strong managerial character . . ., their incorporation of strategically powerful actors, and the opacity of their formal rules and constitutional position." Readers may be tempted to think of these latter networks only as "iron triangles" or agencies captured by interests (cf. Jordan 1981; Makkai and Braithwaite 1991), but we think that they (ironically) resemble a form of representative agency as well.

The power center conjured by Klijn and Skelcher might be created by a form of representative agency that Fung (2003, 345–346) advocates in certain circumstances. He argues for a mini-public characterized by *hot deliberation,* in which deliberators have strong opposing opinions, adversarial debate (designed to convince rather than to compromise), and real stakes – the outcomes of these representative agencies are to be enacted. They essentially produce policy. Fung (2003; 2006) does not take this always to be the best form of deliberation, but he does suggest that, often, it enhances democracy by offering a more representative, deliberative policy-making process, and this by virtue of the fact that it actively involves people from the community in the business of setting local policy.[21]

It is important to recognize that Fung himself remains fairly neutral among public participation schemes. His position with respect to the circumstances in which various levels of public involvement in public policymaking might be appropriate is nuanced (Fung 2003). It seems that his intention lies more in

---

[21] For instance, Fung (2003) says, "[o]n one view, deliberation should be cold. Individuals with low stakes in a discussion will be open-minded, begin without fixed positions, and dispassionate. I tend to the opposite view; hot deliberations with participants who have much at stake make for better deliberation. More participants will be drawn to hot deliberations and they will be more sustainable over time. Participants will invest more of their psychic energy and resources into the process and so make it more thorough and creative. The results of deliberation are more likely to be forcefully supported and implemented" (345).

providing a useful taxonomy of participatory structures, which are more and less commonly used in attempts at more and less collaborative governance, than in making substantive claims about the general desirability of one structure or another (Fung 2006). If we had to describe his substantive position on the matter, we think it is that different circumstances warrant different levels of public involvement. Fung does, however, tend toward championing greater levels of "empowered" public involvement, or *cogovernance*, especially in circumstances in which "a democratic deficit manifests itself as a lack of state accountability or when the minipublic is a component of a governance or problem-solving scheme" (Fung 2003, 346). Careful as he is to attenuate his enthusiasm for such schemes in circumstances where public involvement might produce less than desirable results or constitute a detriment rather than an enhancement to democratic processes, the practitioners following Fung's lead might not be so careful. And what he describes as cogovernance enjoys broad support in public administration (e.g., Bryson et al. 2013; Nabatchi 2012).

Our contention is not that these kinds of governance structures are always a bad idea, but rather that the complementarity principle can be useful to those designing them. Specifically, it is instructive for figuring out when a participatory structure is appropriate and how to design one that promotes responsible policy work. Adherence to the complementarity principle guards against representative agencies that are incompatible with representative democracy, a result which occurs when each (the agency and the democracy in which that agency operates) finds itself operating under a different set of institutional rules (Klijn and Skelcher 2007, 590). Ansell's coolly deliberating advisors, with which we contrast Fung's hotly deliberating policymakers, seems to implicitly follow the complementarity principle, giving it a democratically constrained quality that certain implementations of Fung's model might lack.

Ansell's collaborative governance model adheres to the complementarity principle because it builds the core values of representative democracy into the function of the representative agency. The board, in its advisory role, gives the representative who formed it the information she needs to represent the entire constituency with fidelity by initiating a process designed to draw out the competing concerns and interests on a given public matter as expressed by actual members of the relevant constituency. But, unlike Fung's model of cogovernance directed by engaged and empowered mini-publics, it does this without granting actual policymaking power to the mini-public, thereby (perhaps unwittingly) skirting responsibility or accountability for the policies it makes. Ansell's collaborative governance process does not bypass the collective will; instead, it brings the collective will into greater relief, leaving the representative entrusted with its execution in full control of the relevant policymaking. Note that this process gives the representative the information she needs to determine what a socially equitable outcome looks like in a particular domain, so that she can set up or direct the policy workers on the ground to execute their functions accordingly.

The People's Maps Commission[22] organized by Governor Tony Evers of Wisconsin is an example of cool deliberation in action. The commission met with constituents all over the state, gathered information on demographics, political affiliations, and all manner of other relevant considerations in an attempt to draw up the most equitable, nonpartisan redistricting proposal possible. Upon completion of fact-finding and deliberations, they submitted to the Governor's office what they took to be their best proposals. The office then examined these proposals and chose which one it would submit for approval to the state legislature. This process incorporates the general public in a way that satisfies Fung's (2003; 2006) intuitions about more and less democratic or representative processes in matters of local concern. The Commission also appears to better democratize a process that can and often does result in a serious lack of fairness when executed by people with partisan interests, but it does this in a way that does not delegate powers away from elected officials. The Governor takes the nonpartisan recommendations, decides which among them to submit, and the legislature votes. Absent any evidence of partisan motivations or manipulations on the part of the commission's members or those choosing among their proposals in the Governor's office, the legislature ought to approve the selected map (or at least one among them), since to do so would be to represent the people of Wisconsin with fidelity.

Were it to follow a cogovernance model, the process would be quite different. The People's Maps Commission would simply deliberate and select the map, present that decision to the Governor's office, and in so doing, trigger the relevant redistricting processes to bring the state's districts into conformity with the chosen map. Why might this seem preferable? Just look at what, in fact, happened with this process in Wisconsin. The Governor's office selected the map it deemed appropriate from those submitted by the commission and the map was not only rejected by the state legislature, but the Commission's process was challenged in the Wisconsin Supreme Court. The Governor was obliged to submit instead the map with the least changes as the battle continued to work its way through the courts, and it seems unlikely at this point that the People's Maps Commission will have been able to produce a fair, nonpartisan districting map for the state. The better outcome, one might reasonably insist, is the one in which the map's fairness and accuracy is determined by the nonpartisan

---

[22] https://govstatus.egov.com/peoplesmaps.

commission selected to do the relevant research and map drawing, and that map is imposed on the lawmakers in accordance with the democratic value that "the people ought to choose their representatives, not the other way around" (The People's Maps Commission 2021).

Fung (2003, 345) tends toward hot deliberations with high stakes outcomes like the political geography with which the People's Maps Commission is concerned. He argues that hot deliberation in these cases often results in better outcomes for the people. We argue that those outcomes, even if they are "better" than or preferable to others, are not necessarily more democratic, bypassing as they do the collective will as expressed by the voters in electing the representatives they did. The People's Maps Commission case is especially interesting because it represents something of a Catch 22. The representatives in question were chosen based on the very maps that the People's Maps Commission suggests are unfairly stacked in favor of one party over others, which is unfair *because* it is not representative – according to their data – of the partisan breakdown of the state. This state of affairs makes Fung's model look very attractive indeed, but there must be a better way of alleviating the trouble with these maps than simply putting it to the Commission to replace the existing ones. Why? Because when processes make an end-run around the agreed-upon channels for democratic decision-making, they defy or undermine certain democratic values that the whole redistricting process is supposed to reinforce.

Both Ansell and Fung situate their projects within a system of representative democracy. Because one policy proposal must defeat all others, because people have registered differing opinions about which proposal should be chosen, and because representatives are obligated to take pluralism seriously, the responsive rather than the adversarial model of representation is that which reinforces the political values of the system. In this case, those values are both pluralism and public accountability.

Ansell's responsive, collaborative governance model is designed to reinforce the values of pluralism and the accountability of representatives to the people for two reasons. It takes the voters' will as a starting point for directing public policy, and it uses the recommendations of a group of citizens as more fine-grained data about how best to implement the will of the voters. It facilitates a recursive process of policy goal refinement and explores different implementation options, and all the while, the representative remains accountable to the voters. The model accords with the conjecture that representative agencies can "engage a wider range of actors in the policy process, connecting them in new ways, and thus 'oil the wheels' of representative democracy as it struggles to govern in a complex environment" (Klijn and Skelcher 2007, 594). This is essentially a version of what Fung (2003, 341) calls a participatory advisory panel.

Fung's "empowered" version of representative agency threatens to undercut rather than enhance the value of pluralism by circumscribing a new, narrower "people" – some subset of the voters whose popular will elected the representative – to whom the representative then becomes accountable, thus obviating the value of public accountability. It takes the voters' will as a starting point for directing public policy, then *sets them aside*, allowing the policy implementation decisions to be made by a smaller group of individuals who are selected from the population at large. The representative, on this model, is bound to execute what a mini-public decides, and since the members of the representative agency are not elected, no one is accountable for the outcomes of the policy to the voters. Essentially, the will of the representative agency supplants the will of the broader constituency even if it takes the will of the broader constituency under advisement. Importantly, though, it need not.

According to the criteria specified in Section 2.1, responsible policy work means that wherever possible, policy workers must reinforce the values of the political system of which they are a part. Representative agency structures like those championed by Fung and others in this camp do not necessitate this, and this is because these structures fail to embed complementarity.[23] They do not take seriously one of the major positive obligations of responsible policy work (the capability component), instead directing policy workers to engage in actions that might well run counter to that obligation.

This further illuminates the values that undergird systems of representative government. Responsiveness is necessary for the genuine preservation of pluralism under a representative system. The adversarial model tends to obviate pluralism as a value altogether. Consider the aggressive agendas of straight opposition to the majority party over the past twenty-five years or so in the US Congress. The adversarial stance gives lawmakers strong reasons to decline to represent their constituencies with fidelity, rather, it gives them positive reasons to represent only their own voters – that is, only those who actually voted for them. More insidious still is the fact that once one side has chosen the adversarial model, pluralism is lost. This is so because such an adversarial model is an exercise in anti-democratic, factional people-making. It undermines the democratic value of equal voice – having an equal opportunity to influence public policy.

---

[23] To be sure, Fung (2003) advocates for empowered mini-publics almost exclusively in circumstances in which what we might call "the proper channels of government" have failed or become corrupted. Perhaps, then, his position would more accurately be construed as an instance of non-ideal theorizing than as an ideal form of deliberative democracy. In that case, we still take advocacy of the mechanism to be a pessimistic, perhaps defeatist position.

To insist that policies made by mini-publics (constituted of members of the public and which are, in fact, a subset of the public) rather than by representatives is to confuse *subordinate* values – things like transparency, efficiency, and equity that are valuable insofar as they help to achieve higher, overarching goals – for *bedrock* democratic values like equal voice, maximal public participation, collective decision-making, respect for reasonable disagreement, fidelitous representation, and so forth. Proponents of this kind of model make an inductive inference from the actual outcomes of specific initiatives to the general desirability of the mechanisms that yielded those results. They use inductive normative reasoning to infer a general claim from an existential proposition: Socrates is a man; Socrates is bald; therefore, all men are bald. What "works" or what produces desirable results in a given context does not necessarily improve or enhance democracy – for that matter, what "works" may not turn out to be very democratic at all. It is one thing to claim that deliberative methods (in Fung's [2003] case, using selectively chosen mini-publics in hot deliberations to produce actual policy outcomes) yield better results; it is quite another to claim that without adhering to complementarity they constitute an improvement to or enhancement of the democratic process of policymaking.

5.2 What Makes for a Better Policy?

One final question raised by the foregoing discussion is this: Who decides whether one policy is "better" than another? Pluralism – maintaining the ability of the people to choose and to pursue different reasonable conceptions of the good – is a core value of representative democracy. Because people living in representative democratic political systems have, and are permitted to have, different views regarding what is good or bad, right or wrong both generally and for themselves, differing views about the desirability of public policies (either in general or for someone or some group) are an inevitable consequence of the sociopolitical landscape. Taking questions of public policy to the *demos* as a whole respects pluralism by giving everyone the chance to weigh in on them. Empowering selectively chosen mini-publics to set public policy does the opposite. It makes it possible, for instance, for a select group with certain strong interests to enact policies that run counter to other people's strong interests, thus eroding the value of pluralism. Perhaps it all seems well and good that something like that could happen so long as the decision goes in the way one would like it to go, but that will not always be the case.[24]

---

[24] Within the lore of public administration, consider Thompson's (1972, 621–622) critique of the Minnowbrook conference: "How do you transfer power from those who have it to those who do not? . . . I believe in tolerance, in negotiation and compromise, in contract, in incremental policy making. I do not understand why it has not occurred to the 'New Public Administration' group

Making an end-run around established law-enforcement procedures and standard public accountability measures in order to achieve what many consider a "better" outcome is exactly what the recent Texas anti-abortion law aimed to do (before *Dobbs* v. *Jackson Women's Health Organization* overturned the precedent it was designed to evade).[25] It aligned with certain deeply held beliefs of a large number of Texans, and so constituted, in at least one widespread opinion, a better outcome than having enacted a law that comports with democratic values (like that of pluralism and basic autonomy) and procedures (like the state's enforcement of its own laws). Moreover, this law purportedly democratized the enforcement of law by putting it in the hands of the people. Is that a "better" outcome? And is it – by virtue of putting public decision-making and public law enforcement power in the hands of the people – in fact more democratic or democracy-enhancing? It certainly is not if you consider pluralism to be a core democratic value. It is an instance of minority rule. Designing governance structures that delegate policymaking authority to selected subsets of the public undercuts or erodes pluralism. That is, in failing to adhere to the complementarity principle by designing governance structures with the express goal of reinforcing core democratic values, the Texas anti-abortion law fails to promote or to facilitate responsible policy work. Adopting such governance structures when they are likely to promote "good" outcomes according to your own sensibilities opens the door to legitimizing all such governance structures, whether they get "good" outcomes or not. Hence, our argument focuses on "good" (that is, responsible) policy work rather than on outcomes *simpliciter*. Whatever else one can say about the Texas anti-abortion law, it certainly did not seem to encourage or facilitate responsible policy work.

The solution to the problem of roles and the problem of levels is, at least in part, one and the same: adherence to the complementarity principle in governance structure design. This is why Bertelli (2021, 197) and we connect the criteria of responsibility to the complementarity principle. Part of what determines a "good" or "better" outcome is the aggregate will of the public, or how well the outcomes and the policies and procedures that produce them adhere to the values of the representative democracy of which they are a part.

---

that the governing instrument they wish to create might turn against them and their values and promote a set of values of an entirely different kind."

[25] Senate Bill 8, 87th Leg., Reg. Sess. (Tex. 2021) (S.B. 8) (to be codified at Tex. Health & Safety Code §§ 171.203(b), 171.204(a)). *Dobbs* v. *Jackson Women's Health Organization*, 597 U.S. ___, 79 (2022) held that "The Constitution does not prohibit the citizens of each State from regulating or prohibiting abortion."

6 How Does the Complementarity Principle Function?

EISENHOWER:	*Does that mean that you've changed your mind about leaving the CAB?*
HECTOR:	*No, sir, I'm afraid it doesn't.*
EISENHOWER:	*My powers of persuasion don't seem to be what they once were!*
HECTOR:	*That's not what keeps me from staying. I now worry that the CAB isn't terribly democratic in its processes. I don't want to play a role in derogating democracy.*
EISENHOWER:	*Really, Hector?*
HECTOR:	*The CAB is too independent of you and the Congress. When I arrived, I thought that the answer was to make the CAB more dependent on executive authority.*
EISENHOWER:	*To make me a king, I recall.*
HECTOR:	*Not exactly, but certainly to give you more control over the agenda of the CAB. I now realize that for that control to be democratically exercised, efficiency must be sacrificed, and if that happens, the need for centralizing the control of civil aviation policy in your office becomes less acute.*
EISENHOWER:	*I agree, and not only because it takes something off my plate.*
HECTOR:	*The most important thing I now see, Mr. President, is that the CAB is placing too much emphasis on the messages carried by a few, loud voices – of the passenger airlines and the cities with airports and the manufacturers of airplanes – and it isn't thinking about everyone who is impacted by its policies. I can't fix that from within because I can't do the job by abstaining from it while occupying a seat on the board. It's the structure of our enabling act encourages the problem. To carry out the statute, I must participate in a process that is less pluralistic than our government needs it to be. Congress plainly gave me no alternative.[26]*

---

[26] The U.S. Supreme Court wrote in *Arlington* v. *FCC*, 569 U. S. 290, 296 (2013), that "Congress knows to speak in plain terms when it wishes to circumscribe, and in capacious terms when it wishes to enlarge, agency discretion." The CAB's enabling act states that the "promotion of adequate, economical, and efficient service by air carriers at reasonable charges, without unjust discriminations, undue preferences or advantages, or unfair or destructive competitive practices" serves the public interest, 52 Stat. 980 (1938).

EISENHOWER: *That is a very principled act, Hector, but are you sure you can't do something from your seat on the board?*[27]

HECTOR: *Suppose that I were an artillery officer and that there was a coup d'etat being waged against you.*

EISENHOWER: *Not the happiest hypothetical I have ever been given by a lawyer!*

HECTOR: *I apologize, Mr. President, but bear with me. Suppose it were my job to drive a tank, and that I had been directed by my superior officer, who was with the plot to oust you, to drive that tank right up to the Executive Office Building and point it at the Indian Treaty Room with the intent of deterring you from making a statement on television that might galvanize opposition to the coup.*

EISENHOWER: *Go on.*

HECTOR: *As I see it, I have only one course of action available to me. To preserve democracy, I must stop the tank, get out, and leave my commission behind. I cannot recreate the hierarchy of authority of the Army from my seat in the tank, nor can I preserve the values of our democracy by remaining there.*

EISENHOWER: *So, you're getting out of the tank?*

HECTOR: *And I will write an article explaining to Congress how it can draft better legislation to regulate civil aviation.*

EISENHOWER: *You're a man of integrity, Hector.*

HECTOR: *I'm a responsible administrator, Mr. President.*

The final premise in the argument for the indispensability of the complementarity principle is that the complementarity principle directs institutional designers to keep the relevant political values and their reinforcement in mind. The purpose of this section is to explain how it does this.

The complementarity principle functions in two ways. First, it positively guides governance structure design in a way that ensures responsible policy work by directing designers to embed value reinforcement mechanisms into rules, procedures and organizational characteristics. Second, it counteracts the

---

[27] Reflecting on cases where the U.S. Supreme Court rejected claims of administrative discretion from which the majority in *West Virginia* v. *EPA,* 597 U. S. ____ (2022) a "major questions doctrine," Justice Kagan wrote: "First, an agency was operating far outside its traditional lane, so that it had no viable claim of expertise or experience. And second, the action, if allowed, would have conflicted with, or even wreaked havoc on, Congress's broader design. In short, the assertion of delegated power was a misfit for both the agency and the statutory scheme" *West Virginia* v. *EPA,* 597 U. S. ____ (2022) at 13 (Kagan, J., dissenting).

potential for irresponsible policy work in governance mechanisms that were not expressly designed with value-congruity in mind by forestalling the kinds of errors that tend to result from the use of normative inductive reasoning as outlined in Sections 2.3 and 2.4. That is, it provides a general principle that can be consulted by rank-and-file policy workers whenever novel normative discretionary situations arise.

On Bertelli's (2021) view, the central normative issue of public administration is responsibility.[28] His position rests on a forward-looking view of representation as a mechanism for overcoming factionalism by acting according to the expressed desires of one's constituents (179), a view which we have fleshed out and called fidelitous representation.

> To be responsible, policy workers must use their discretion to serve public aims. These aims are expressed and articulated formally through the mechanisms of representative government – elections, representation, legislation, oversight, the rule of law. To be responsible, policy workers must use the capabilities they have – and those they can get – as well as their judgments and informal actions to serve public aims as effectively as possible within the limits of the law. (Bertelli 2021, 175)

The complementarity principle guides the design of governance structures such that they facilitate or encourage responsible policy work in accordance with this forward-looking view of representation by embedding an ethos of value reinforcement into public administration. Specifically, the values to be reinforced are those of the political system within which the agency or the individual policy worker performs a specified function. At its most general level of description, the complementarity principle says: *Governance values ought to complement political values* (Bertelli 2021, 197).

Where this principle is followed, governance structures are intentionally designed to serve their *governments* rather than their own internal aims, the aims of any particular officeholder within their governments, or any foreign influence. To illustrate this point, Bertelli (2021, 189–196) uses the example of an executive who hopes to suppress voter turnout by enacting a voter identification law. He works through a number of scenarios as to how the law might be carried out by policy workers in administrative agencies that differ in their governance structures. Since the values of representative government are those

---

[28] Compare responsibility defined as Bertelli (2021, 170) does below with the view of Rothstein and Teorell (2008) that "democracy in the form of political equality on the input side must be complemented with impartiality on the output side of the political system, that is, in the exercise of public authority" where impartiality means, "When implementing laws and policies, government officials shall not take into consideration anything about the citizen/case that is not beforehand stipulated in the policy or the law." Impartiality in their view is more like a Dworkinian rule, but responsibility is a broader a normative principle.

to be reinforced by responsible policy work, and since representative governments value universal suffrage, the policy workers, when acting responsibly, coordinate their efforts at their (legally circumscribed) discretion to ensure that every eligible voter has access to the requisite voter identification. In so doing, they implicitly abide by the complementarity principle. Bertelli also gestures in the case of each kind of agency at what irresponsible policy work might look like in such a scenario. Doing so draws out the importance of designing governance structures in accordance with the complementarity principle.

Absent an explicit, guiding design principle, public administration systems and individual public administrators may or may not demonstrate value-congruity in their day-to-day operations. Where they do, it is by accident. Recall the distinction between representative agencies that incorporate cool or hot deliberation. Both models complement the democratic value of collaborative self-governance, but only the cool deliberation version maintains accountability on the part of elected officials by designing the agency with deference to the collective will – as expressed by the democratic mechanism of the vote – and fidelitous representation. The hot deliberation mechanism at best sidesteps and at worst undercuts these (and other) values by relying on what Lafont (2020) describes as a "shortcut" through the democratic process. As we argued in Section 5, this model sets aside the voters and effectively replaces them with a mini-public whose shrunk-down, demographically (or less) representative will supplants the expressed will of the broader constituency. Whether we describe it as merely sidestepping or effectively undercutting the democratic values of universal participation, equal voice, collective will, and fidelitous representation, hot deliberation used widely threatens to *weaken* these fundamental values of representative government.

Ansell's (2011) version of the same kind of agency, however, does not have the same deleterious effects. He champions the model of representative agency he does perhaps because of an implicit belief in something like the complementarity principle. Our contention is that a certain uniformity of value-congruity across all levels and systems of governance is perhaps achievable by making the complementarity principle *explicit* as a standard normative guideline for designing governance structures, the result of which is a public administration workforce that administers democracy. Embedding value-congruity into what it means for a public agency to function properly both encourages and facilitates responsible policy work according to the characterization we developed, articulated, and defended in Sections 2 and 3. Where this express guidance is lacking, institutional designers might well be wasting their time and energy sketching out undesirable governance structures – that is, governance structures that, however unintentionally, permit or encourage irresponsible policy work. In the case of representative democracies, such policy work fails to administer democracy each and every day.

To be sure, many methods intended to identify the values that ought to guide public administration ultimately shortcut core democratic values of the state. Consider Moore's (2014) contention that policy workers "should earn their keep by creating public value." He describes two types of public values. The first denotes values as public because they "focus on the welfare and just treatment of others," society could promote them or not (468). The second are public by virtue of being "articulated and embraced by a polity working through the (more or less satisfactory) processes of democratic deliberation to guide the use of the collectively owned assets of the democratic state" (468). Both definitions capture contestable values, and values of the second type are democratically generated articulations of what the people value, but they are not themselves democratic values. Suppose a state's institutions are majoritarian. If Moore's public value determined what democracies value, or what democratic values *are*, then building the public administration from contestable social values would allow for (shifting) majority views to say what democracy is and is not, and what it does and does not value. Moore supplies no corrective should values like equality be undermined as majority-endorsed outcomes accrue "public value" on his ledger. In recognizing the core values of democracy as the normative basis on which the public administration ought to be built, adherence to the complementarity principle safeguards against possibilities like the ones Moore leaves open.

The second way that the complementarity principle functions is to provide active guidance to street-level policy workers who routinely encounter situations that require normative judgment calls to be made at their professional discretion. Rather than adhering to an all-or-nothing doctrine regarding the permissibility of the use of unfettered normative discretion, policy workers can weigh possible courses of action against the backdrop of the political values of the system in which they operate and make informed determinations about how best to proceed. Decisions made on these informed grounds are, importantly, more likely to be consistent with one's own prior and subsequent professional judgment calls, as well as those made by others in similar positions, than they would be if everyone was obliged to make such calls according to their personal values (or barred from making such calls at all).

Notice how its two-fold function allows the complementarity principle to bridge a certain gap between ideal and nonideal theorizing.[29] It constitutes an

---

[29] Rawls (2001) distinguished between ideal theory and nonideal theorizing on the basis of compliance with the principles of justice, or on the basis of whether or not a society is a perfectly just one. Nonideal theorizing concerns principles for action under conditions of

instance of ideal theory insofar as it provides a standard at which to aim when designing governance structures. At the same time, though, it constitutes an instance of nonideal theorizing because it provides guidance that is applicable at the moment of decision-making so that policy workers can strive toward the ideal even in the nonideal circumstances in which they find themselves. It gives real public administrators a way to make authorized normative judgments in their daily professional lives. By contrast, Zacka (2017, 48–65) argues that certain facts about the personal moral lives of street-level bureaucrats coupled with the fact that they must make normative discretionary judgments in their professional capacities renders the "rational systems perspective" or "compliance model" of public administration unfeasible; the complementarity principle offers guidance to address those legitimate feasibility concerns.[30] We agree that street-level bureaucrats have to use normative discretion. The complementarity principle we propose offers a way to specify the relevant values according to which professional normative judgments should be made *and* directs institutional designers to build the reinforcement of those values into governance structures so that these kinds of decisions will be less ambiguous (because they are not unguided) from the moment they arise.

---

merely "partial compliance" where certain injustices do and will continue to prevail while ideal theory assumes "strict compliance," guaranteeing a fully just society in which people universally comply with the principles of justice.

[30] Zacka (2017, 247) says that "no normative theory of the state would be complete that did not attend to the process of policy implementation in some detail and to the agents responsible for it" and that "[w]e need a more thorough political theory of implementation." His study is intended to contribute to that project by showing that the rational systems perspective of public administration is inadequate, given certain facts about how policy implementation actually works. Worth noting here is that Zacka places his project squarely in the realm of non-ideal theorizing. He specifies at the end of the first chapter that his conclusions are reached holding fixed the way bureaucracies operate today, including the assumption that where normative discretion is employed, decisions are made in accordance with one's personal values *and* the assumption (which he, we think rightly, contests) that normative discretion at the street-level is undesirable. The complementarity principle offers an ideal for guiding normative discretion that runs counter to the first assumption and thus in part answers one of his major feasibility concerns about the compliance model that we have argued is basically correct. He says that "[i]n the absence of the goal specificity promised by the rational systems perspective, street-level bureaucrats *have no choice but to set their own ends*, within the scope of reasonable construals" (63, emphasis added). The "goal specificity" in question is supposedly promised by a hierarchical control model which is meant to obviate normative discretion at lower levels of administrative systems. Attending to value-congruity is, in a sense, an alternative to the hierarchical control model he has in mind. It obviates the need for street-level bureaucrats to set their own ends by providing them with an applicable set of values *and* the reasons why that set of values ought to supersede their own in their professional discretionary decision-making processes. An empirical question that remains open is whether adherence to the complementarity principle in governance structure design would actually lead street-level bureaucrats to reinforce political values rather than making decisions according to their own values in practice. This (among others) is a question Bertelli intends to investigate in a large-scale project (details are available at https://repgov.eu).

7 Conclusion

If we have successfully argued our case in each of the previous sections of this essay, the conclusion of the argument for complementarity follows. Those who design governance structures ought to adhere to the complementarity principle. Our fictional dialogue between President Eisenhower and Louis Hector illustrates the consequences of not doing that in terms of administrative behavior.

In support of the first premise, that responsible policy work requires workers to reinforce the political values of the system in which they operate, we have given a justification for adopting Bertelli's (2021) substantive view of responsible policy work. On this view, responsible policy work has an *individual duty*, a *rule of law*, and a *capability* component that work together to guide action. In the process, we identified and explicated a set of core democratic values, and showed how these connect with conditions of responsibility for both representatives and everyday policy workers in representative democracies. While this was a lot of conceptual ground to cover, going to the trouble enabled us both to clarify several aspects of our project and to contribute to scholarship about public administration, public policy and politics by supplying a concrete set of concepts that might be of use going forward.

The second premise states that since responsible policy work requires workers to reinforce the political values of the system in which they operate, governance structures ought to be designed with the relevant political values and their reinforcement in mind. To support it, we have articulated a general view of the values of representative democracy, defended the claim that regime changes and other major political shifts must not be executed by policy workers acting in their capacities as policy workers, and argued for the preferability of fidelitous representation over pursuits of social equity at the unguided discretion of policy workers. We have shown that unguided pursuits of social equity by policy workers are not necessarily desirable, and that they are not strictly necessary for achieving equitable outcomes so long as the representative democratic value of fidelitous representation is respected, and so long as deference to this and other democratic values is embedded in systems of public administration.

In support of the third premise, we have reiterated what the complementarity principle is and how it serves as a normative guide to good governance structure design and good (responsible) policy work. To illustrate its function, we contrasted two similar governance structures, one which does and one which does not adhere to the principle, and we have argued that making the principle explicit would better enable governance structure designers to create the kinds of agencies that, through their daily operations, administer democracy. We have argued that complementarity acts as a bridge between the very nonideal circumstances in which we find ourselves and the democratic ideals toward which we aspire, and that it does this without relying on shortcuts that threaten to weaken the core values of representative democracy.

In theory, adherence to the complementarity principle in governance structure design should contribute to the betterment of democracies insofar as it aims them toward better realizing their own fundamental ideals. More generally, when governance structures reinforce the values of the political systems of which they are a part (that is, *any* political system), when their functions are executed responsibly, the systems are optimized and their stability and sovereignty are safeguarded. This, we contend, is preferable for those living out their daily lives under any kind of regime to a system in which instability reigns. While democratic systems very well may be preferable to those which fail to respect basic human rights or support human flourishing, these injustices are only exacerbated by irresponsible policy work on the part of policy workers within such regimes, who are supposed to be working on behalf of those regimes. Perhaps this means that responsible regime change ought to take place outside of the official operations of government, as our fictional Hector's hypothetical about the *coup d'etat* – or the real choice facing Soviet officers outside the "Russian White House" in August 1991 – exemplifies. Likewise, policy workers in authoritarian systems would not act responsibly if they became agents of regime change on behalf of foreign governments. We think that actions like these misconstrue the problems of roles and levels that we have discussed, and they allow the choices of policy workers to supplant democratic political action. We are inclined to at least tentatively endorse this conclusion in the absence of any argument to the contrary. What remains to be seen is whether empirical research that considers the characteristics of democracy rather than policy outcomes supports it.

References

Ansell, Christopher. 2011. *Pragmatist Governance: Re-imagining Institutions and Democracy*. New York: Oxford University Press.

Bertelli, Anthony M. 2016. "Who Are the Policy Workers and What Are They Doing? Citizen's Heuristics and Democratic Accountability in Complex Governance." *Public Performance & Management Review* 40(2): 208–234.

Bertelli, Anthony M. 2021. *Democracy Administered: How Public Administration Shapes Representative Government*. New York: Cambridge University Press.

Bertelli, Anthony M., and Madalina Busuioc. 2021. "Reputation-Sourced Authority and the Prospect of Unchecked Bureaucratic Power." *Public Administration Review* 81(1): 38–48.

Bradbury, Mark, and J. Edward Kellough. 2011. "Representative Bureaucracy: Assessing the Evidence on Active Representation." *American Review of Public Administration* 41(2): 157–167.

Bryson, John M., Kathryn S. Quick, Carissa Shively Slotterback, and Barbara C. Crosby. 2013. "Designing Public Participation Processes." *Public Administration Review* 73(1): 23–34.

Carpenter, Daniel P. 2001. *The Forging of Bureaucratic Autonomy*. Princeton, NJ: Princeton University Press.

Carpenter, Daniel P. 2010. *Reputation and Power*. Princeton, NJ: Princeton University Press.

Cooper, Terry L. 1998. *The Responsible Administrator*. 4th ed. San Francisco, CA: Jossey-Bass.

Cordelli, Chiara. 2020. *The Privatized State*. Princeton, NJ: Princeton University Press.

Dworkin, Ronald. 1990. *Law's Empire*. Cambridge, MA: Harvard University Press.

Engster, Daniel. 2020. "A Public Ethics of Care for Policy Implementation." *American Journal of Political Science* 64(3): 621–633.

Estlund, David. 1990. "Democracy without Preference." *The Philosophical Review* 99(3): 397–423.

Frederickson, H. George. 1971. "Toward a New Public Administration." In *Toward a New Public Administration: The Minnowbrook Perspective*, edited by Frank Marini, 309–331. Scranton, PA: Chandler.

Frederickson, H. George. 1980. *New Public Administration*. Tuscaloosa, AL: University of Alabama Press.

Frederickson, H. George. 1990. "Public Administration and Social Equity." *Public Administration Review* 50(2): 228–237.

Fung, Archon. 2003. "Recipes for Public Spheres: Eight Institutional Design Choices and Their Consequences." *The Journal of Political Philosophy* 11(3): 338–367.

Fung, Archon. 2006. "Varieties of Participation in Complex Governance." *Public Administration Review* 66 (s1): 66–75.

Goodsell, Charles T. 2011. "Mission Mystique." *American Review of Public Administration* 41(5): 475–494.

Hart, H. L. A. 1961. *The Concept of Law.* Cambridge, MA: Oxford University Press.

Heath, Joseph. 2020. *The Machinery of Government: Public Administration and the Liberal State.* New York: Oxford University Press.

Hector, Louis J. 1960. "Problems of the CAB and the Independent Regulatory Commissions." *Yale Law Journal* 60(6): 931–964.

Hobbes, Thomas. 1668. *Leviathan.* Edwin Curley, ed. Indianapolis, IN: Hackett.

Hofstadter, Douglas. 1981. "A Coffeehouse Conversation on the Turing Test." *Scientific American* 244: 15–36.

Jordan, A. Grant. 1981. "Iron Triangles, Woolly Corporatism and Elastic Nets: Images of the Policy Process." *Journal of Public Policy* 1(1): 95–123.

Joyce, Kathryn E., and Nancy Cartwright. 2020. "Bridging the Gap between Research and Practice: Predicting What Will Work Locally." *American Educational Research Journal* 57(3): 1045–1082.

Kilpatrick, Carroll. 1973. "Nixon Forces Firing of Cox; Richardson, Ruckelshaus Quit: President Abolishes Prosecutor's Office; FBI Seals Records." *Washington Post.* October 21.

Kingsley, J. Donald. 1944. *Representative Bureaucracy: An Interpretation of the British Civil Service.* Yellow Springs, OH: The Antioch Press.

Klijn, Erik-Hans and Skelcher, Chris. 2007. "Democracy and Governance Networks: Compatible or Not?" *Public Administration* 85(3): 587–608.

Lafont, Cristina. 2020. *Democracy without Shortcuts: A Participatory Conception of Deliberative Democracy.* Oxford: Oxford University Press.

Levinson, Meira, Tatiana Geron, and Harry Brighouse. 2022. "Conceptions of Educational Equity." *AERA Open* 8(1): 1–12.

Locke, John. 1689. *Two Treatises of Government.* Peter Laslett, ed. Cambridge Texts in the History of Political Thought. New York: Cambridge University Press.

Long, Norton. 1952. "Bureaucracy and Constitutionalism." *American Political Science Review* 46(3): 808–818.

Makkai, Toni, and John Braithwaite. 1992. "In and Out of the Revolving Door: Making Sense of Regulatory Capture." *Journal of Public Policy* 12(1): 61–78.

McFadden, Robert D. 2019. "William Ruckelshaus, Who Quit in 'Saturday Night Massacre', Dies at 87." *New York Times*. November 27.

Meier, Kenneth J. 1975. "Representative Bureaucracy: An Empirical Analysis." *American Political Science Review* 69(2): 526–543.

Moore, Mark H. 2014. "Public Value Accounting: Establishing the Philosophical Basis." *Public Administration Review* 74(4): 465–477.

Mosher, Frederick C. 1968. *Democracy and the Public Service*. New York: Oxford University Press.

Nabatchi, Tina. 2012. "Putting the 'Public' Back in Public Values Research: Designing Participation to Identify and Respond to Values." *Public Administration Review* 72(5): 699–708.

New York Times. 1973a. "Excerpts from Transcript of Cox's News Conference on Nixon's Decision on Tapes." *New York Times*. October 21.

New York Times. 1973b. "Ziegler Statement and Texts of Letters." *New York Times*. October 21.

Noble, Kenneth B. 1987. "Bork Irked by Emphasis on His Role in Watergate." *New York Times*. July 2.

O'Leary, Rosemary. 2010. "Guerrilla Employees: Should Managers Nurture, Tolerate, or Terminate Them?" *Public Administration Review* 70(1): 8–19.

The People's Maps Commission. 2021. "About the People's Maps Commission." https://govstatus.egov.com/peoplesmaps/about.

Rawls, John. 1999. *A Theory of Justice*. Cambridge, MA: The Belknap Press of Harvard University Press.

Rawls, John. 2001. *Justice as Fairness: A Restatement*. Cambridge, MA: The Belknap Press of Harvard University Press.

Raz, Joseph. 1986. *The Morality of Freedom*. New York: Oxford University Press.

Raz, Joseph. 2006. "The Problem of Authority: Revisiting the Service Conception." *Minnesota Law Review* 90: 1003–1044.

Raz, Joseph. 2009. *The Authority of Law*. Cambridge, MA: Oxford University Press.

Riccucci, Norma M., and Gregg G. Van Ryzin. 2016. "Representative Bureaucracy: A Lever to Enhance Social Equity, Coproduction, and Democracy." *Public Administration Review* 77(1): 21–30.

Rosenbloom, David H. 2005. "Taking Social Equity Seriously in MPA Education." *Journal of Public Affairs Education* 11(3): 247–252.

Rothstein, Bo, and Jan Teorell. 2008. "What Is Quality of Government? A Theory of Impartial Government Institutions." *Governance* 21(2): 165–190.

Rousseau, Jean-Jacques. 2019. *On the Social Contract*. Donald A. Cress, trans. Indianapolis, IN: Hackett.

Saltzstein, Grace Hall. 1979. "Representative Bureaucracy and Bureaucratic Responsibility." *Administration & Society* 10(4): 465–475.

Schouten, Gina. 2019. *Liberalism, Neutrality, and the Gendered Division of Labor*. New York: Oxford University Press.

Shelby, Tommie. 2007. *We Who Are Dark*. Cambridge, MA: The Belknap Press of Harvard University Press.

Svara, James H., and James R. Brunet. 2004. "Filling in the Skeletal Pillar: Addressing Social Equity in Introductory Courses in Public Administration." *Journal of Public Affairs Education* 10(2): 99–109.

Thompson, Victor A. 1972. "Review of *Toward a New Public Administration: The Minnowbrook Perspective*, by F. Marini." *American Political Science Review* 66(2): 620–622.

Young, Iris Marion. 2000. *Inclusion and Democracy*. Cambridge, MA: Oxford University Press.

Williams, Brian. 2014. Inside the Mind of Edward Snowden. NBC News. May 28.

Zacka, Bernardo. 2017. *When the State Meets the Street: Public Service and Moral Agency*. Cambridge, MA: The Belknap Press of Harvard University Press.

Zacka, Bernardo. 2022. "Political Theory Rediscovers Public Administration." *Annual Review of Political Science* 25: 21–42.

Acknowledgments

Bertelli acknowledges the support of an Advanced Grant from the European Research Council (grant agreement no. 101020966). We thank José Luis Martí, Josep Joan Moreso, Meira Levinson, Andrew Williams, Ben Jones, Desirée Lim, Norma Riccucci, Silvia Cannas and seminar participants at Pompeu Fabra University, the University of Padova and the University of Barcelona for helpful comments and suggestions.

Cambridge Elements ☰

Public and Nonprofit Administration

Andrew Whitford
University of Georgia
Andrew Whitford is Alexander M. Crenshaw Professor of Public Policy in the School of Public and International Affairs at the University of Georgia. His research centers on strategy and innovation in public policy and organization studies.

Robert Christensen
Brigham Young University
Robert Christensen is professor and George Romney Research Fellow in the Marriott School at Brigham Young University. His research focuses on prosocial and antisocial behaviors and attitudes in public and nonprofit organizations.

About the Series
The foundation of this series are cutting-edge contributions on emerging topics and definitive reviews of keystone topics in public and nonprofit administration, especially those that lack longer treatment in textbook or other formats. Among keystone topics of interest for scholars and practitioners of public and nonprofit administration, it covers public management, public budgeting and finance, nonprofit studies, and the interstitial space between the public and nonprofit sectors, along with theoretical and methodological contributions, including quantitative, qualitative and mixed-methods pieces.

The Public Management Research Association
The Public Management Research Association improves public governance by advancing research on public organizations, strengthening links among interdisciplinary scholars, and furthering professional and academic opportunities in public management.

Cambridge Elements

Public and Nonprofit Administration

Elements in the Series

CPSIA information can be obtained
at www.ICGtesting.com
Printed in the USA
BVHW050803180123
656507BV00015B/166